MEXICO

Como México no hay dos
There are no two like Mexico

MEXICO

Text by Walter Hanf
with 50 Color Plates

RAND McNALLY & COMPANY

Translated by Eamonn J. Doyle

The printing blocks were produced by Brend'Amour, Simhart & Co., Munich. The illustrations were printed by Stadlerdruck, Constance, on Rotafolio manufactured by the Schnellpressenfabrik Koenig & Bauer, Würzburg. E. C. Baumann KG, Kulmbach, typeset and printed the text. The paper was provided by Heinz Uhlemann KG., Eltville. The binding was done by Grossbuchbinderei Sigloch, Künzelsau.

In the Shadow of the Volcanoes

Alfonso reined in his horse. "Now we have to continue on foot, *Señor*."

I asked myself if it were possible to continue at all. As in the legend, the Glass Mountain towered in front of us. Black lava stretched across the countryside. Pitted blocks of basalt heaped upon each other ten, fifteen, twenty yards high by the volcano's rivers of fire, formed a bizarre black slag heap.

My Indian guide knew a path, and as we halted for a rest by a ruined church in the middle of the lava field, he recounted the history of Paricutín, Mexico's youngest volcano.

"It was on the twentieth of February, 1943. A farmer called Dionisio Pulido was plowing his cornfield when he heard a noise like thunder and noticed a long but shallow fissure between the clods of earth. At first he didn't bother about the unusual occurrence, but after a while the ground swelled inside an existing hole in the field. A cloud of gray dust rolled out of the ground, and there was an odor of sulphur. An uncanny rumbling and quaking began, and finally Dionisio ran terror-stricken to the village of Paricutín.

"We knew Dionisio, *Señor*. He was a quiet man with nothing of the humbug about him, but at first no one wanted to be taken in by the story of the smoking cornfield. Eventually, however, we decided to take a look, and you can imagine our horror when we saw how Dionisio's field was gradually disappearing. It was being swallowed by an enormous hole that spewed out stones, sand, and smoke. Later we were told that we were the first witnesses of an historical event. We had seen what had never before been granted to human eyes in Mexico: the birth of a volcano."

Alfonso paused and passed his hand reflectively over the sparse stubble of his beard. He had certainly given this account a thousand times or more — it was, after all, his profession — but he seemed to have been so impressed by the performance of the subterranean powers that he shuddered with the retelling.

"Then, *Señor*, hell really broke loose. The eruptions of the volcano came faster and faster. Rocks weighing tons, glowing lumps of basalt as large as houses, shot out of the crater. Smoke rose miles into the sky and everything was covered in ashes. The earth bellowed and raged and could be heard for miles around. The volcano grew hour after hour. Lava rolled over our fields and woods. Our village disappeared, and only this church, as you can see, remained standing."

In fact, its massive walls rose out of the lava field like the church steeple out of the man-made reservoir that I had once seen in Austria. Lava has completely filled the church aisle and one tower has burst apart, but the altar, side walls, and clock-tower have withstood the white-hot stones. "This was a miracle for us," said the Tarasco Indian simply, "the miracle of our altar-piece, *Santo Cristo de los Milagros*. And if you had seen that inferno, you too would understand why we believe it a miracle."

Even without believing in miracles I could understand Alfonso easily. Only a few weeks earlier, in the Central American coffee republic of Costa Rica, I had witnessed the spectacular activity of the volcano Irazú. It also growled and, at short intervals, hiccuped a cloud of stones and ashes from its maw. It stank of sulphur, as if the devil himself had slipped through the earth's chimney. Before the wind could clear away the clouds of dust and vapor, Irazú exploded a new load of ash across the land. And this land was one of the most desolate that I had ever seen. Buried knee-deep in ash, it was dark and dead. No grass waved in the breeze, no bird sang; the trees were black skeletons. Not even the echo of one's footsteps was to be heard; the shoes sank silently into the dust. It was like a moonscape.

These, then, are the volcanoes, and the Mexicans live with them on very familiar terms.

They are a dramatic element in the Mexican landscape. Quenched and cold, but by no means lifeless, as the constant earthquakes remind us, the chain of cone-like peaks runs from the north through the Mesa Central, reaches its highest summit at 18,429 feet in the Pico de Orizaba, casts its gigantic shadow from Popocatépetl and Ixtacihuatl over the capital, Mexico City, blusters through Guerrero and Oaxaca, forms the restless and smoldering backbone of the Central American causeway, and surges on to join the South American Andes. The earth is restless, and the people live in the shadow of the volcanoes.

A fire-spewing mountain is, however, not the only feature that can lend drama to a landscape. Mexico also offers breathtaking contrasts completely free from smoke and ashes. In the northwest, for example, the *Sierra Madre Occidental* has ripped the land into gorges, precipices, caverns, waterfalls, and river-courses of primeval savagery. The *Barrancas del Cobre,* the copper gorges, drop hundreds of yards and, with seven side valleys, form a system of canyons that is one of the mightiest and most inaccessible in the world. Altogether, the canyons are estimated to have a length of 1,250 miles; the wildness and impenetrability of the terrain so far have prevented an accurate land survey. Few of the canyons are accessible for the mountain climber, and then only along dizzying goat tracks. Even the journey by rail through the *Sierra* of Chihuahua to Los Mochis on the Pacific can only be recommended to those unaffected by dizziness. The train climbs the mountain wall like a caterpillar, forces itself slowly out of the abyss, and sways free on one of the fifty bridges above the illimitable depths. Seventy tunnels thrust their way through this primeval world — a territory which for centuries had tolerated only the Tarahumara Indians and which had resisted the railroad for almost seventy years, from 1897 to 1961.

Westward from Los Mochis on the mainland, across the Californian Gulf, lies Lower California, the dangling drop on the Mexican cornucopia. This part of California begins the *savannas,* the plains of grass and cactus that are the habitat of the *vaquero,* the Mexican cowboy, and his herds of cattle. The scenery should be well-known to every moviegoer, for without it the Wild West film could not exist. The United States border can hold back the desperado but not the cactus, the sisal, and the salt deserts that Texas and Chihuahua, Arizona and Sonora have in common. A landscape as burning hot as thirst itself.

Another hot, arid, and burning landscape is the low-lying eastern coast on the Gulf of Mexico, where the ports of Tampico and Veracruz conjure images of petroleum, waterfront taverns, Caribbean rhythms, Hernán Cortéz, freebooters, film heroes, adventure and danger. Yellow fever, once the greatest danger presented by these steaming lowlands, has almost disappeared. Since Cortéz landed in Veracruz, the two murderers, malaria and yellow fever, had claimed hundreds of thousands of victims. Anyone forced to live in the tropical lowlands and in the rain forests and mosquito swamps of the Gulf once was all but condemned to death. The white man could best live and survive in the perpetual spring of the uplands — in Mexico City, Puebla, Guadalajara, Taxco, Morelia, or Guanajuato — where pine and oak woods, mountain fields, and meadows exude a cool, clear air. Lake Chapala smiles and the waters of Lake Pátzcuaro are an invitation to bathe.

The way southwest from the plateau to the Pacific leads through a landscape once described very graphically by Hernán Cortéz in a letter to Charles V of Spain. So that the king could visualize the terrain of his new colony, Cortéz advised him to crumple a sheet of parchment in his hand and release it; then he would have Mexico before his eyes.

The view of Acapulco Bay is captivating. The bathing resort and film city rises from the waves of the Pacific, a shimmering necklace of elegant hotels along its sandy beach. The one-time small colonial port offers a facade of luxury and frivolity that nevertheless hides a dirty backyard.

To the south, the Isthmus of Tehuantepec is one end of an audacious engineering plan to connect the Atlantic and Pacific Oceans by building a canal through the narrowest part of Mexico. However, the canal project does not seem to be immediate and Tehuantepec continues to doze. The women, their dress, and their songs possess a melancholy beauty.

A magnificent superhighway leads further south to Tapachula. On the roof terrace of the *Restaurante Mil Tortas,* the restaurant of a thousand cakes, the coffee planters rattle their dominoes as if it were possible to conquer the heat with noise. The air vibrates and shimmers like the air above a blast furnace.

Again we have contrasts. Directly behind Tapachula on the southwestern tip of Mexico, *the Sierra Madre de Chiapas* finally rises to 9,186 feet — to pine woods and tangled forest inhabited by Indians — and gently curves eastward through Campeche to the peninsula of Yucatán. A calcareous plain is what the geologists term the cradle of the Mayan culture.

1   View of Ixtacihuatl (left) and Popocatépetl (right) across Mexico City

8   *In the Museum of Anthropology and History, Mexico City*

"The area produces almost half the world's sisal," say the economists in their professional tone.

Sisal grows abundantly in Mexico, but for the most part the cornucopia shape of the country is a deceiving symbol. In an area almost the size of Western Europe, some forty million people subsist on the yield from one-seventh of the land. The other six-sevenths is either too wet or too dry, too hot or too cold, too mountainous or too wooded for cultivation. Lying along the same latitudes as Cairo, Delhi, Senegal, Madras, and Manila, Mexico would be a warm-to-tropical country were it not for its mountains and plateaus. Instead, temperatures range from hot in the *tierra caliente* lowlands, with an annual mean reading of 75° F., to a cold zone at an elevation of about 15,000 feet, and the weather varies from snowstorms on Popocatépetl, through sandstorms in the *llanos* of the north, to cyclones in Mérida. Mexico possesses a great variety of terrain, vegetation, and climate; only in arable land is it deficient. Truly, "*Como México no hay dos*," there are no two like Mexico; but neither is Mexico all one.

Fallen Civilizations

The ancient gods have a new abode, after four hundred years of persecution, destruction, and disdain. The Mexican government has built them a palace without equal in the world: The National Museum of Anthropology and History. The period spanned by the museum's collections is enormous. It is the historical epoch that modern Mexico has rediscovered and, above all, given a new life, in order to create for itself a historical heritage. After three hundred years of feudal domination by the Spaniards and a century of oligarchical independence, *la nueva raza* was born of revolution — the new spirit of free Mexico. This new Mexican, however, must understand that he is the heir to advanced civilizations of his own which were on a par, if not superior to the Spanish conquerer's Christian-Western culture. The Anthropological Museum in Mexico City's Chapultepec Park provides him with proof, knowledge, and conviction in equal amounts. It is a grandiose, illustrated history book of his heritage. The government's intention in building the museum palace is expressed in newspaper articles that celebrated the opening of the museum on September 15, 1964.

"All our current efforts to make Mexico a great nation must avail themselves of our past. A people that does not foster respect for its history an traditions will never be a great people." Thus the Anthropological Museum becomes a supporting witness for the *grandeza Mexicana*.

The museum has so clearly and vividly arranged the immense time span from the first traces of human beings in Central America to the arrival of Hernán Cortéz that even the foreigner receives a concise overall view of the diversity of the ancient Mexican civilizations. Here under one roof he finds at a glance a range of cultures, which in origin were scattered across thousands of miles and hundreds of years: The plateau civilizations of Teotihuacán, Tula, Xochicalco; the Olmec mother civilization of the Mexican Gulf in La Venta and Tres Zapotes; Monte Albán and Mitla in Oaxaca; Uxmal, Chichén Itzá, Palenque, and Bonampak in the territory of the Mayas, which reached as far south as Guatamala, El Salvador, and Honduras. Here in the museum is a fascinating panorama of religions and civilizations that already were advanced cultures when Rome in the Old World was ruled by the soldier-emperors, when Origen and Ulfilas were writing their theses, and before the kingdom of the Franks had been founded. The American "savage" was at least partially the contemptuous invention of the conquerors who sought to justify their own misdeeds.

When we take a stroll as members of a conducted museum tour, the first thing we sense is the mystery of the ancient Mexican civilizations. Where did the original inhabitants of the continent come from? Perhaps they crossed the Bering Straits in exodus from Asia to Alaska, migrated southward, and established agricultural settlements.

The history of Mexican civilization began with the Olmecs, between 1500 and 800 B.C. The Olmecs worked in jade, basalt, rock crystal, and quartz. From these materials they carved colossal heads with Negroid features, deformed and close-shaven skulls, blunt noses, and protruding lips. They left masks, jewelry, tools, and laughing statuettes, which are curious exceptions in the stern pantheon of the ancient Mexicans. It has been established that the Gulf coastal area was the home of the Olmecs, of which La Venta and Tres Zapotes are the architectural legacy, that they were ruled by priests, sorcerers, and shamans, that they filed their teeth to points, played ball games, and had developed a script and a calendar with eighteen months.

Nothing more is known about the Olmecs. They vanished about the beginning of the Christian era. But their influence can be traced through all the later civilizations: Zapotec, Toltec, Maya, and, finally, the Aztec.

When the Roman Empire was passing its zenith, the uplands of Mexico witnessed the flourishing of a civilization whose remains are as plentiful as its origins are mysterious. The pyramid city of Teotihuacán lies only a short distance from Mexico City. Even for the Toltecs, who occupied Teotihuacán around A.D. 1000, the pyramid city was a phenomenon, as it also was for the Aztecs who arrived later. In both languages the name means "place where the gods live." The gigantic pyramids seemed simply inconceivable as dwelling places for ordinary people; superhuman beings must have lived here. Even the Spaniards seemed to believe in the myth of the giants of Teotihuacán, and as proof Cortéz sent Charles V some gigantic bones. The bones were later identified by archaeologists as being quite terrestrial; they had once run through Mexico as the legs of mammoths.

Archaeologists so far have been unable to discover the origins of the Teotihuacán Empire. Since the founders of Teotihuacán evidently cremated their dead, no revealing artifacts of their culture have come from graves. The script has also defied all attempts at translation and interpretation up to the present. However, the sporadic excavations begun in the middle of the last century have given way to systematic research, but the answer to the riddle is still a long way off. This was confirmed by Mexican archaeologist Ponciano Salza Ortegón, whom I asked while in the pyramid city to describe the separate stages of history of the Teotihuacán Empire.

"We are still unable to establish exactly the individual stages with respect to time," said Salza Ortegón. "The experts are working on three hypotheses, which I should like to call the extreme, the moderate, and the conservative. The extremists, if I may say so, believe it probable that the city was already founded about 600 B.C. The moderate theory places the founding of the city in 100 B.C., while the conservatives favor the year A.D. 400. Just about all the researchers are unanimous that the Teotihuacán Empire went into decline about A.D. 700 and that it had reached its pinnacle within its last four hundred years."

"Do you believe that it will ever be possible to reconstruct and explain the history of Teotihuacán completely?"

"If we wanted to investigate thoroughly all the buildings and historical periods, then we would still have at least fifty years of research ahead of us. We have therefore concentrated on the latest stages of civilization. Of course we are extremely careful during the excavations so that we will later be able to investigate the earlier periods. Our first aim, however, is to restore the frescoes and the so-called Pyramid of the Moon."

The Pyramid of the Moon takes on an almost ethereal appearance beside the mass that later generations called the Pyramid of the Sun. Human hands piled up 1,310,000 cubic yards of stones in an effort to get closer to the gods, step by step. For this is the magical meaning of the Mexican pyramids. Their steps formed the bridge to the gods, and 365 steps, one for each day of the year, lead to the platform on the Pyramid of the Sun, which towers 207 feet above the landscape of the gods. This platform once supported a temple and a massive piece of sculpture, which were destroyed by the Spaniards immediately after their arrival.

The steps on the Mexican pyramids, together with the temples and sacred statues on the platforms, are evidence that the pyramids in Mexico were not constructed as funeral vaults or monuments to the dead, as were those in Egypt. The pyramids were always only pedestals for the places of worship where the people communed daily with their gods in the face of the sun. Whether they sacrificed, prayed, sang, or danced — they always were closer to heaven and the living world than to the realm of death, to which the people of Teotihuacán by no means accorded the same morbid significance as did the Egyptians.

If one views Teotihuacán from the platform on the Pyramid of the Sun, the design with which the city was laid out is clearly recognizable. Various centers of worship or residence arose, interconnected by two main thoroughfares and several lesser streets. The Street of the Dead stretches two and a half miles to the Citadel (these erroneous names are based on previous misconceptions), which is again formed by a self-contained system of smaller pyramids.

In the Citadel, however, the main pyramid, consecrated to Quetzalcóatl, literally gives a comprehensive cross section of the religious conceptions and the architecture of the people of Teotihuacán. Two pyramids appear to have been built one behind the other, but in fact one is on or in the other. The rear (upper) pyramid is fitted over the front (lower) one. Only a part of the outer "shell" has been removed from the upper pyramid, and as a result the lower one stands out. This cross section also shows a facade of the lower pyramid that is symbolically decorated with 365 ornaments portraying the feathered snake Quetzalcóatl and the rain god Tlaloc.

But why did the Mexicans fit their pyramids one over the other? Like all the advanced civilizations of America, the people of Teotihuacán believed in the perpetuation of the world by cyclical renewal. When a cyle of fifty-two years had ended, everything had to be renewed: houses, pottery, temples. New pyramids were built over the old ones — until the gods moved out. And this is what they did in Teotihuacán around the year 900. The temple city in the upland valley of Mexico, constructed in honor of the rain god Tlaloc ("heavenly seed"), was already empty when the Toltecs came.

The origin of the Toltecs is obscure and their exit from history equally mysterious. It is believed that they ruled one, possibly several, empires from A.D. 300 to 1000, and that their territory reached from the tablehand to Tabasco on the Gulf. The Toltecs were the first real imperialists of old Mexico. They pursued an expansionist policy and inflicted a merciless, bloody, sacrificial theocracy on their neighbors. They were, however, brilliant architects and astronomers.

The pyramid of Cholula, for example, is thought to be Toltec. With a base measuring four times 1,312 feet, it is the largest edifice of this type in the world. It now rises out of the plain as a hill overgrown with trees and bushes, and a Catholic church occupies the spot where the temple of Quetzalcóatl once stood.

The Toltecs also migrated southward, and Toltec remains and influence had already been discovered in Maya territory when the scholars were still arguing about the existence of their royal city of Tula. It was only in the 1940's that archaeologists decided to excavate near the city of Tula de Allende, in the southern state of Hidalgo. They discovered the legendary center of the Toltec Empire, its pyramids, and towering steles.

The Chichimecs were the successors of the Toltecs. Whether they expelled the latter or just filled the vacuum left by a voluntary departure is as unclear as the reasons for the migrations of the Olmecs, Mayas, Zapotecs, and Mixtecs. Mexican schoolchildren don't have to bother themselves with lists of dates when studying their ancient history. Loose ends and theory are a large part of their education, in contrast with the European high schools where the study of Western culture entails an accurate chronology.

The origins of the Zapotec civilization on Monte Albán near Oaxaca, whose history is thought to stretch back to the era of Teotihuacán, the pyramid city, are also obscure. The Mixtecs brought the immense temple complex of Monte Albán under their domination and expanded the Zapotec burial center Mitla ("place of the dead") into an administrative capital. The Mixtecs had also vanished before the "floating houses" of the Spaniards were sighted off the coast of Veracruz.

The rise of one of the most highly developed cultures, the Maya civilization, which reached its zenith between A.D. 300 and 900, is also a subject for speculation. It has been called the Maya Empire, although no proof exists that Yucatán, Chiapas, Belize, Guatemala, and parts of El Salvador and Honduras were ever governed from a common capital. On the contrary, diverse politico-religious centers in these areas indicate that individual empires, tribes, and city-states developed separately — comparable with the European national states under a general Christian hegemony. Another factor that tends to refute the existence of a giant empire is the observation that nowhere among the Maya are found any traces of an aggressive and imperialistic military dictatorship, such as that perfected later by the Aztecs in central Mexico.

We can reconstruct the style of clothing worn by the Maya Indians, what they ate, how they lived, what they believed in, and the language they spoke, and much of this can still be observed today among the two million direct descendants of the Mayas. We know that the ancient Mayas had matchless mathematicians and astronomers, who were acquainted with the zero figure centuries ahead of the Arabs and Assyrians. Their calendar, which was derived from observations of the planetary system, and probably the solar system within the Milky Way, was superior to our calendar. The Maya year contained 365 days, 5 hours, 48 minutes, and 28,8 seconds, so that the calendar had to be corrected by a leap year only three times in then thousand years. The Maya had worked out and given names to time spans of three million years. They had a script that we can only partially decipher. Their art, according to Paul Westheim, is "feudal art, an American baroque that develops into a captivating rococo, the creation of a feudal society whose passions were art and science." Over a hundred major Mayan cities were scattered through the lowlands of Mexico and Guatemala. These were not cities in the modern sense, however; instead, they were related clusters of communities. The sites uncovered in the Guatemalan jungle, at first mostly by European and American archaeologists, were Chichén Itzá, Palenque, Uxmal, or Petén. They appear to have been temple cities of the priestly oligarchy, around which lay people lived in villages.

A million Indians are estimated to have lived in the Maya territories during the classical period. Sometime around A.D. 900 they stopped building and abandoned their lands, and the advanced civilization declined. This decline is currently thought to have been internal: the result of hunger, drought, plague, or overpopulation. Later, with the coming of the Toltecs, the Maya experienced a renaissance, the so-called New Empire, which lasted until the assault of the Spaniards. Its center lay in northern Yucatán, mainly in Uxmal and Chichén Itzá. The Spanish Bishop Diego de Landa, who had ruined priceless relics of the Maya culture when he was a young priest, only to restore them later as an old bishop, said that Chichén Itzá "was equally as holy for the pilgrims of that time as Jerusalem is for the pilgrims of today."

Chichén Itzá means "Mouth of the Spring" (chi: mouth; chén: spring). Itzá was the name of a Maya tribe that had founded the city in the sixth century. The city's name is significant. Possession of a spring or well was essential in ancient Yucatán. Water was life. Yucatán is a limestone plain with neither rivers nor lakes, and rain immediately sinks into the porous earth to collect in underground watercourses that emerge later on the surface as isolated oases, called *cenotes* in Mexico. *Cenote* is, however, the Spanish word for the Maya spring — at best a small pool but in most cases only a water hole. The community grew up around the well and was nourished by it. The *cenote* was so closely united with the peoples' existence that it often assumed a holy significance and function. Like the people of Teotihuacán, the Maya also worshipped a water deity, identical with the god of fertility. The Holy Spring, *cenote sagrado* as it was called by the Spaniards, is circular, 174 feet in diameter and 82 feet deep, and lies between steep limestone walls.

The temple of the rain god Yum-Chaca is at the edge of the pool. When the land was threatened by drought the rain god received a human sacrifice, and the ceremony is illustrated in the frescoes of the temple. At sunrise a beautiful maiden was painted blue, the sacrificial color, and led blindfolded to the temple of Yum-Chaca. She was accompanied on the way by priests, musicians, singers, and dancers, who had roused themselves to the necessary ecstasy with *balche*, a sacred drink. After the prayers had been pronounced, the songs had been sung, and the dances had been danced, the maiden was thrown into the pool from the temple platform. Precious jewelry, articles of everyday use, and images of the god were thrown in after her to strengthen the petition for rain.

In 1894, the former American Consul-General in Yucatán, Edward Thompson, was so intrigued by the legend that he had divers investigate the sacrificial well. They brought up curious dolls, bits of skeletons, and other objects. Since then the well has been systematically dredged for its sacrificial offerings.

In the Old Empire, the "Golden Age," the architecture had developed into a captivating,

9   *Celebration in Honour of the Virgin of Guadaloupe, Mexico City*

cheerful rococo. Palenque, Tikal, Copán, and Petén were enlightened centers of culture, where religion complemented art and science. The Chichén Itzá of the Toltecs was stricter and more totalitarian in government and religion, and the architecture was no longer cheerful. Compared with the extravagant ornamentation of the Old Empire, the Temple of the Tiger, the Warriors' Temple, and the ball court of Chichén Itzá are severely classical in construction. Subjection to the gods had become more absolute and fanatic. The gods, however, were bloody, immediate, and ubiquitous. They manifested themselves even at the ball game, which was no longer a sport, but a religious act and divination.

Two teams took the field at Chichén Itzá in the name of the gods. They played along a 82-foot long stone wall, which had a stone ring attached to it at a height of about 13 feet. The ring was placed with its mouth vertical to the playing field and not horizontal, as in basketball. The two Maya teams of seven players each propelled a solid rubber ball high up the wall with their elbows, hips, or knees. If the ball flew through the ring a team had shot a "goal." The fourteen players ran and jumped as if their lives were at stake, which, in fact, was the case. The victors would chop off the heads of the vanquished, for the result of the game was sentence, divine will, and oracular decree.

The earthly representatives of the gods dominated the subjects in every aspect of life. They were the absolute lords over life and death, and gave the New Empire the character of a totalitarian theocracy. Keith Botsford called Chichén Itzá, "the capital city of a sanguinary and unpleasant people, which finally became a city of wizards, mathematicians and calendar-makers, a city no longer fit for human habitation. Both state and religion evidently became metaphysical abstractions which were based on rigid laws and iron authority. Such inflexibility and inability to adapt ended in self-destruction."

Whether or not self-destruction was the cause, Chichén Itzá already stood empty when the Spaniards arrived. A large number of the Maya Indians had retired to the uplands of Chiapas and Guatemala. They still live there today, speaking their ancient language and practicing their ancient customs, isolating themselves from the modern state that is attempting to integrate them into society, not with violence, but with patience and persuasion.

The ethnology section of the Anthropological Museum gives insight into the everyday life of the modern Maya Indian. This everyday life has probably not altered in thousands of years, neither for the Maya nor for the Zapotecs, Otomi, and Tarahumara.

33

Suddenly the twilight and obscurity are lifted from Mexican history. The Aztecs enter the picture, warlike, predatory, and aggressive. It was quite some time before the nomadic tribe developed into the expansionist nation of conquering warriors whose empire collapsed in the clash with the Spaniards. The Aztecs abandoned their nomadic existence in 1325 and settled on an island in the Anáhuac uplands, where they founded Tenochtitlán, "the place where a cactus stands on a rock." On this cactus they had seen the eagle with a serpent in its beak and, according to the vision of the priests, this indicated the place where they should build a permanent home. This is what the legend says, and the coat of arms of Mexico, the eagle, serpent, cactus, and rock, embody the legend.

Once they had settled down, the Aztecs quickly subjugated their neighbors, exacted tribute, and engaged in permanent warfare against the rest of their world, justifying themselves ideologically by claiming that their sun god Huitzilopochtli had an insatiable appetite for prisoners of war. When the priests wanted to bring about a religious war they would exhort the people with "the Sun is almost dying of hunger." Through these wars the "People of the Sun" eventually stretched from the Pacific in the west to the Gulf in the east and southward to what is now the Republic of Guatemala. The Aztec capital, Tenochtitlán, previously a collection of reed huts, became a magnificent metropolis, where the Spaniards in 1519 noted a population of around 300,000.

We now know the details of life in the Aztec capital. We know the political, social, and religious laws, the educational system, the social structure, the layout of the markets and streets of Tenochtitlán. An exact model of the City of the Sun has been constructed, Diego Rivera has painted scenes from the city in gigantic frescoes, and in the Anthropological Museum there are showcases in which details of clothing and of fruit in the marketplace are reproduced.

Bernal Díaz de Castillo, the chronicler of the Spanish *Conquista*, described the "Mexican Venice" that he viewed from the upper platform of the Pyramid of the Sun:

"We saw beneath us three highways that led to Tenochtitlán and the aqueduct that came from Chapultepec and provided the entire city with fresh water.... The lake was alive with watercraft bringing foodstuffs, consumer goods, and other merchandise to the city. From this viewpoint it was also easy to see that the inhabitants could only go from one house to another by means of drawbridges or boats. Everywhere arose the white, glistening sacrificial temples, towers and fortified castles above the tops of the residences to form an admirable and picturesque view."

The order and discipline of the Aztec capital was imposed by a despotic religion that had degenerated into a cult of blood by the time the Spaniards were announced to Montezuma, the last of the Sun Kings. Under the influence of his priestly advisers, Montezuma believed that the Spaniards were the returning gods. He saw in the captain Hernán Cortéz the white god Quetzalcóatl, a Toltec king revered as a god who had wanted to do away with human sacrifice and who, according to legend, would one day return from the sea in the east. It was this superstition, and not the cannon, horses, and lances of the conquerors, that was disastrous for the Aztecs. One of the most daring and adventurous *coups de main* in world history overwhelmed a well-armed military and police state, which had been crippled by the decree of a religious oracle. In addition to this, Cortéz was an excellent officer and diplomat who understood how, through military alliances, to utilize to full advantage the hatred of the Aztecs' plundered neighbors. One of the main factors contributing to the defeat of the Aztecs was the use of Indian auxiliary troops by Cortéz, Indians who fought for their freedom from the Aztec yoke only to be enslaved by the conquistadores.

But Montezuma is not yet vanquished and Tenochtitlán not yet captured:

Good Friday of the year 1519 or, by the Aztec calendar, the year "Thirteen Rabbits": The Spaniards are sighted off the coast.

The year "One Pipe": The Spaniards come to the Palace of Tlayácac.

Montezuma sends Cortéz priceless gifts and has him dressed in the garments of the god Quetzalcóatl. Cortéz makes a pact with the tribes that are suffering under the Aztec terror and marches with a group of five hundred men and the Indian "Legionnaires" from Veracruz to Tenochtitlán, undergoing terrible hardships on the way.

The year "One Pipe," month "Bird," day "Eight Wind": The Spaniards enter Tenochtitlán.

Montezuma receives Cortéz as a god. The Sun King is held as a hostage by the Spaniards, surrenders the fabled Aztec golden treasure to them, submits to them, but refuses baptism. Cortéz has to leave the Aztec capital to intercept a punitive expedition sent by the governor of Cuba, Velázquez, who wants to bring the unruly captain to his knees. Cortéz defeats his compatriots, returns to Tenochtitlán, and finds the city in complete uproar. During his absence his deputy Pedro de Alvarado has caused a frightful bloodbath among the noble warrior caste. He has massacred the unarmed Aztecs during a religious ceremony — simply cut them down. Cortéz tries to restore order, but Montezuma is stoned to death by his outraged people. The Spaniards flee, losing many of their soldiers and much of their equipment. The state treasure of the Aztecs sinks into Lake Texcoco and is lost forever. All this occurs in the night of June 30 to July 1, 1520: *la noche triste*, the night of grief. Even Cortéz is said to have wept.

The Spaniards, in the meantime, do not abandon their quest. They recruit new mercenaries and are back within a year. Tenochtitlán, defended by the young Aztec King Cuauthémoc, is besieged by Cortéz for eighty days. Cannons kill 240,000 Aztecs! On August 13 the city falls and is razed by the besiegers. Bernal Díaz has written: "Now everything lies scattered on the ground and not a stone remains standing on another."

The Indians poets mourned the fate of their city in much the same dirge-like tones as the ballad singers of today at the corridas. Barely two years after the destruction of Tenochtitlán an unknown singer was lamenting in his mother tongue, Náhuatl:

> The walls are black,
> Smoke blackens the air;
> Only the deadly fire gleams in the dark.

> They have captured Cuauhtémoc,
> The Princes of Mexico are captives.
> Ah, how true it is
> That they who once were kings
> Are now but captives.

> What can still be done, my friends?
> The Aztecs are leaving the city,
> Smoke veils the horror,
> And our city stands in flames.

Weep, my friends, and understand:
The Mexican Empire is lost.
The water has become bitter,
And bitter is the food.

Only flowers and dirges still remain
In Mexico and Tlalteloco
Where once we saw warriors and sages.

Thoughts in the Plaza of Morelia

It is always the same. Where the two main streets cross, there lies the *plaza*, the little square in the heart of every Mexican town. The great city, the little town, the market village, the hamlet with its church, all are subject to the architectural conventions of the Spanish — to the square. All of them cluster around the *plaza*.

Nearly each *plaza* is the same. The Holy Trinity of an immovable social order fixed for eternity. Here stands the church — one side of the plaza for the church. The headquarters of the local civil authorities take up the opposite side. The square is closed by the residences of the gentry, and the basic plan of the Iberian world picture is complete. Variations change nothing, for the variances among *plazas* are only size, rank, and wealth of the individual communities; but never the basic plan. Whether gleaming baroque towers soar into the sky, as in the silver town of Taxco; whether the presidential palace fronts a square that is bigger than St. Peter's in Rome, as in Mexico City; whether burros graze before a wretched wooden church and the guardian of the peace sways gently in a hammock — all of this has no significance. The pattern is monotonous; it is repeated a thousandfold. Variety has been stifled by the Spanish convention. One town is every town and every town is Spanish. The basic plan of Mexico is Spanish.

The journey from Mexico City to Morelia over an immaculate superhighway lasted six hours by luxury bus. And now I am sitting — where else? — on an iron bench in the *plaza* of Morelia, the capital of the state of Michoacán. I could just as well be sitting in the plaza of Puebla, Cuernavaca, or Veracruz, for in activity and rhythm they all merge into the *one* great main square of Mexico.

The plaza is always animated. The local gentry succumb to a carefully nurtured boredom, have their shoes cleaned, leaf through the local newspaper or magazine, ward off with a sovereign gesture of the left forefinger the horde of peddlers — flowers, peanuts, chewing gum, fruit, ice cream, hats, clothes, holy pictures, safety pins (who could ever examine the whole range of a Mexican peddler's wares?) — engage in emotional discussions with acquaintances, rattle their dominoes, and study the lottery tickets of the blind ticket seller. They go as they come, without apparent reason.

The Indian family squats in the grass and eats its travel provisions, with red lemonade as a special treat. Indians are always sitting and eating in the grass on the *plaza*. The children are quiet and dignified, with faces from an archaic age and eyes as black as obsidian.

The guardian of the peace struts in spurred boots across the *plaza* of Morelia, a revolver dangling from his belt and stern awareness of his authority apparent on his face. In the center of the *plaza* is a cast-iron pavilion, as much a part of the Spanish convention as the church and the town hall. Here, on Sunday, the brass band of the volunteer fire brigade serenades the town. Pairs of young girls, clad in tulle and lace and demure smiles, take their promenade around the square to meet the young lads of the town strolling in the opposite direction. Two circles pass each other by, touch each other with their eyes, and probe with half-concealed innuendos. Hour after hour it goes on, round after round, always in opposite directions and always under the strict and watchful eyes of the matrons who sit with their sewing in their laps and meditate on the Sunday *paseo* of their own youth. The *plaza* is the embodiment of eternal recurrence. The evening sky soars above the cathedral and the governor's palace.

Is the atmosphere deceptive? Of course it is! I am sitting in the *plaza* of Morelia in the second half of this century and my neighbor is eating a pork chop wrapped in a newspaper that reports something or other about missiles. The shoeshine boy is wearing a sweater with the words *"Segura Social"* written in big letters across the front. He is demonstrating for social welfare. The Sunday procession of the young people fulfills its social function. It costs even less than a cinema ticket or a visit to a dance hall. Nevertheless, participants in this interplay of eyes are getting fewer and fewer. They are being drawn to the sports grounds and youth clubs that today welcome even the poorest of the poor. The youth of Mexico are abandoning the Spanish customs more easily and naturally, and are adopting a more cosmopolitan way of life.

For two pesos a newsvendor sells me a plain, unadorned guidebook that promises me the sights, *los lugares de interés*, of Morelia. And there it is: the regional museum. How could it be otherwise? One only has to scratch at the surface of Mexico and revealed immediately are fragments of pottery, rags of cloth, and skulls. In the regional museum of Morelia the past of this part of Mexico is cataloged, and relics are on display that give some idea of the daily life, social structure, and symbols of the Tarascan Empire. Until they were razed by the Spaniards, the temple cities of the Tarasco monarchy held their own even against their hostile neighbors, the Aztecs.

The Tarasco pyramids were among the most impressive constructions of the pre-Cortéz civilizations until they, too, fell victim to the Christianizing zeal of the padres. Tarasco government and administration were on a high level, until the Indians were forced by colonial bureaucracy into bonded-servitude and menial labor. All that remains are customs and language, seen and heard in the *plaza* of Morelia where the Indian family squats over its meal. Perhaps they have traveled for over a week, these Indians, from their cold mountains in the *tierra fría*. They have descended only to light a candle to the Black Virgin of Guadalupe in her church.

The guidebook has already enlightened me about the church of Guadalupe. It would be unthinkable for it not to exist — a place of pilgrimage, colonial baroque, built in 1716, yet by no means one of the oldest churches. Sixteen years after Hernán Cortéz had destroyed the capital of the Aztecs, Morelia, or Vallodolid as it was then called, was granted a city charter by royal decree. By 1531, the Franciscan Father Antonio de Lisboa had built a church here in the city and had begun the work of trying to curb the savage harshness of the Spanish conquest. One of the cruelest of the conquistadores, Nuño de Guzmán, had occupied the Tarasco city of Michoacán, and the Indians had fled to the mountains before his inconceivable brutality. Only after their safety had been guaranteed by the priests would they consent to return and settle down under the protection of the church.

One can raise many reproaches against the Spanish Catholic Church, and the Mexicans never spare their reproaches, but without the humane influence of the missionary orders the people, along with the old Mexican cultures, would have succumbed to the gold-greedy soldiery. Beside such brutes as Nuño de Guzmán or Pedro de Alvarado (even Cortéz is a noble figure compared with them) stand missionaries like Bartolomé de los Casas and Vasco de Quiroga as apostles of a human compassion. The Indians survived because of the conflicts between the Crown, the church, and the Spaniards on the scene, each of whom had a different objective and in their conflicts, Indians benefited. However, for the millions of Indians living isolated in jungles and mountain valleys, geography was their true salvation. Even so, a frightful decimation of the people could not be prevented.

Thus it was that the forerunner of present-day Morelia, an Indian community, grew up around the church. Eleven monasteries were founded, one after the other. Between 1640 and 1744 arose the cathedral that occupies one side of the *plaza*. The economic activities of the first inhabitants were almost exclusively connected with the churches and monasteries, but gradually the secular buildings of the Spanish colonial officials took their places in the center of the town. These officials built themselves a Sevillá or a Cádiz in Morelia, but at the same time they developed a nationalistic pride based on Mexico's geographic position as the center of a gigantic colonial empire. The administrative scope of the viceroy of New Spain extended from San Francisco (California) in the north to the Isthmus of Panama. *La grandeza Mexicana* was the pride of the *nouveaux riches*.

Shortly after their arrival the Franciscan fathers founded a college that today competes with Santo Domingo and Lima for the place of the oldest university in the New World. Even this university has now forgotten that it was once a center of Spanish scholarship and theology. Like most of the universities in Mexico it has become a gathering point for the "barefoot and shirtless" heirs of the revolution that broke the dam of social privilege in education, setting free a stream of intellectual activity and ideas.

Radicalism is not new to the students here. The history of the University of Morelia parallels the history of Mexico, for the school was always a center of plotting and conspiracy against the Spanish, the French, the Americans, and local tyrants. The school was founded by Bishop Vasco de Quiroga, a man revered by the modern state as no other colonial prince ever was. The Indian villages around Morelia are still operated according to the bishop's plan of a moneyless, near-communist economic structure four hundred years after their creation. This man also founded the University of San Nicolás in 1540, which was closed from 1810 to 1847 while students and professors were fighting for Mexico's independence from Spain. Between 1864 and 1867, the imperial interregnum of Maximilian, the authorities again shut down the school. When the Mexicans were carrying out the first great revolution of this century in 1910, the students were once again at the barricades.

Priests also fought against the Spanish throughout the war for Mexican independence. Two of them, Miguel Hidalgo and José María Morelos, were closely connected with the University of San Nicolás, and local patriots proudly call their town "the cradle of Mexican freedom." Miguel Hidalgo, who proclaimed independence and led the peasant bands against the Spanish garrisons, was a professor at the university. Both he and Morelos, his student and friend, paid the penalty for his sedition before a Spanish firing squad. As both renegade Spaniards and excommunicated priests, they felt the full vengeance of the colonial church, bureaucracy, and oligarchy.

Five years before Karl Marx was born, Morelos had written:

"The enemies of the nation shall be the rich, the nobles and the highest-ranking officials..." Then comes the list of demands that has retained its significance for the Mexico of today: national sovereignty; freedom from monopolies; the power of the state to be exercised by the people, who would choose its representatives by free election; foreigners to be tolerated as long as they served the national welfare; no slavery or differences between classes; the rule of law; no legal punishment by torture; the inviolability of private property. Although this was written in 1813 its ideals are only partially fulfilled today.

At midnight on September 15, 1810, the pastor of the poor, Miguel Hidalgo, tolled the bell in the little town of Dolores, shouted *Mexico — viva Mexico*, his famous cry of freedom, and with Captain Allende, led the rising against the Spanish. It was not until 1821, however, that Mexico finally separated itself from the Spanish motherland, only to crown General Augustin Iturbide — Emperor Augustin. The emperor was shot shortly afterwards. In Mexico the heartbeat of history has often sounded like the crack of firing squads.

Mexico was now free, but for the poor people nothing had changed. The Spaniards, the great landowners, church property, corruption, favoritism in public office, poverty, and the demands of the revolutionaries still were there. Dictators came and went like the seasons in

42

a renaissance procession of intrigue and unrest, political murder and bandit conspiracy, organized violence, blood, and adventure. One dictator deserves to be described in more detail: the *Caudillo*, General Antonio López de Santa Anna, whose leg, shot off in the battlefield, was enshrined in the cathedral at Mexico City by his orders.

Santa Anna was a monster, scoundrel par excellence. If he hadn't existed in bloody reality Hollywood would have had to invent him and his scenario: how he drove his country to economic ruin through irresponsible financial policies; how he had the American defenders massacred at the Alamo during the first fight for Texas; how he, when a prisoner, hid under a blanket in terror; how he handed over half the territory of Mexico to the Americans for a nominal payment; how he had himself honored as a human god.

The reaction of the people was not long in coming. Out of the turbulance strode a great and earnest personality, President Benito Juárez, who is revered by the Mexicans as a reformer and constitutionalist. Juárez' achievements are bound up with the unique phenomenon of faith and church in Mexico.

The year is 1857. In Morelia, the first gas lamp has just begun to burn, and it illuminates a peacefully sleeping little town. Its pale light is deceptive, however, for even in Morelia Juárez liberals stand opposed in deadly enmity to the conservative landowners and the church. Civil war breaks out and Juárez has to flee to the United States. Napoleon III sends a Hapsburger, Grand Duke Ferdinand Maximilian, to Mexico as emperor. When the new ruler passes through the triumphal arch in the capital with his consort he reads on a banner: "Eternal fidelity to the Emperor of Mexico, Maximilian, and his gracious spouse, the Empress Carlotta."

Where Morelia was concerned, my little guidebook indicates the wall against which the republican martyrs faced royalist firing squads. Maximilian also fell before the executioners' rifles; the "eternal fidelity" had lasted all of three years. But the guidebook was silent about the death site of the royalist supporters of Maximilian.

With Maximilian the Mexican ruling class became French. Under the dictator Porfirio Díaz, 1877 to 1911, the country went through a phase that expressed itself in a thoroughly French manner. Sevillá and Cádiz were no longer in vogue, and the upper classes adopted the new fashions. Architecture that is not colonial Spanish in the center of Morelia is colonial French, but not Mexican.

Porfirio Díaz ruled for thirty-four years. Although politically and economically capable, he became corrupted by power. In the eyes of the world Mexico developed from a comic-opera state into a stable nation that gave rich returns for economic investment. Foreign capital flowed in large quantities into the country for the first time, and the dictator organized a sale of Mexican land that reached huge proportions. Almost one-fifth of the territory was sold to foreigners. The local landowners became *latifundistas* by acquiring enormous estates as large as European duchies. With their *rurales,* bandits in the uniform of the provincial police, the *latifundistas* terrorized the peasants and chased hundreds of thousands from their small farms. Thereafter 97 percent of Mexico's rural population possessed no land. Tens of thousands of political prisoners, and those sentenced to deportation, languished on the sisal plantations in Yucatán and in the forests of Quintana Roo. Beneath the smooth surface of the first Mexican economic miracle a sullen resentment smoldered. The historian Jesús Silva Herzog wrote: "All this gave the occasion for the rising of the people when the first cry for freedom and justice was given. The light of hope burst out anew in the hearts of the poor." What came was *la Revolución.*

On the "Street of No Reelection"

Two of Mexico's states have been named after great historical figures, Hidalgo and Morelos. And Mexico has honored its reformer Benito Juárez by giving his name to the town, Ciudad Juárez. For most streets, bridges, and schools, however, the people of this country reserve other commemorative names. *Avenida Insurgentes,* cutting through Mexico City, is dedicated to the insurgents of 1810. The most beautiful boulevard of the city sparkles in honor of Juarez' reforms, *Paseo de la Reforma.* The date of independence is also the name of a street, *16 Septiembre.* Parallel to the *Avenida Juárez* runs the strange-sounding Street of Article 123, named for the constitution. Another street sign proclaims the strictest principle of young Mexico: *Calle de Noreelección.*

With "No Reelection" as their slogan, on September 27, 1910, the liberals rose against the eighty-year-old dictator Porfirio Díaz, who still showed no willingness to release Mexico from his grasp. The time was ripe for revolution, however, and a chaotic, spontaneous, uncoordinated explosion took place as the Mexican people lashed out against everything that reminded them of the past: against the continued imitation of Europe, against the semi-feudal landholding system, against the preferred positions of the Catholic Church, the army, the foreigners, and the government officials permanently in power. Leaders emerged from the masses. Emiliano Zapata in the south, under the banner of "Land and Liberty," led peasant armies. Pancho Villa, the ex-bandit in the north, led cavalry which overwhelmed the government troops and marched into the capital city. General Venustiano Carranza led the revolt in the northeast, Alvaro Obregón in the northwest. Mexico was ablaze with revolution. In 1911, Francisco Madero became president, but peace did not return to Mexico. Madero was murdered and the supporters of Díaz took over Mexico City. In 1913, led by General Victoriano Huerta, the forces of the past tried to stop the revolution; they failed and a long struggle began.

The chaos of revolution assumed gigantic dimensions. The Zapatistas fought against the Villistas and both against the Carranzistas. Mexico was aflame. Hunger, disease, lawlessness, and violence afflicted the unhappy people, as the machinery of the state came to a standstill. At one time three presidents were in office, two of whom formulated their own laws, and their own army, and printed their own banknotes. The third, Pedro Lascurain, probably holds a record political eclipse in that he lasted all of fifty-five minutes as president of Mexico.

Carranza became president, and when he tried to install a friend as his successor, a revolt began, and he was murdered while fleeing to the coast. Zapata refused to capitulate, was tricked, and assassinated. Villa surrendered, retired to a country estate, and was killed. Obregón became president, tried to flout the law against reelection, and was murdered.

Plutarcho Calles became president. He attempted to enforce the anticlerical laws of the constitution, and revolt flared again, especially in the conservative states of Jalisco Michoacán, Colima, and Puebla, as the faithful rose against the persecution of the church.

When President Lázaro Cárdenas took office in 1934, the spilling of blood that had cost over two million lives came to an end. The revolution had reached and passed its high point. Cárdenas was the first to redeem the promises of the constitution that was written in 1917 and proclaimed as the basis of social justice for all Mexicans. He effected land reforms and came into conflict with the United States and Great Britain when he nationalized the oil fields and railways. Mexico had taken another step on the way toward national autonomy. Today, as the still influential grand old man of Mexican politics, Cárdenas manages a power plant in Michoacán. Presidential assassinations have come to an end, and all of Cárdenas' successors who have not died a natural death are still in the service of the "permanent revolution." In Latin America, with its eternal *coups d'état* and military revolts, this fact alone is sufficient proof of Mexico's stability. In fact, President Cárdenas made a sensation when he said: "The Mexicans will have to get used to the idea of being governed without violence."

Mexico still stands with one foot at the starting point of its revolution: The social contrasts are almost as great as before. A middle class is gradually growing, but vast areas of the country remain isolated and await deliverance from a medieval form of life. Land reform is progressing slowly; it is unprofitable and its most daring projects are succumbing to an explosive increase in population. Even the most impressive work of postrevolutionary Mexico, the fight against illiteracy, threatens to be swamped by the avalanche of people. With an annual increase of 3 percent, or about one million people, Mexico's present population of 40 million is expected to double by the end of the century.

Income in parts of the country has remained static since 1934 in spite of a 500 percent increase in the national income. In addition to the new class of industrial magnates, bankers, and state officials, those who profit most from the rapid growth of new industries are mainly the inhabitants of the industrial centers: Mexico City, Guadalajara, and Monterrey. On the other hand, there are in Chiapas, tens of thousands of Indians who have not even entered a money economy. About 50 percent of the Mexican population lives fairly well and can be called "modernized". Some are poor and some are rich, but this 50 percent eats fairly well, is educated, lives in a modern economy, has modern housing. The other 50 percent lives about as its ancestors did. The achievement of the revolution is that the percent living in the modern world went from 10 to 50.

Nevertheless, Mexicans continue to challenge hard reality with their unshakeable belief in progress. They set all their hopes on the "permanent revolution." Untiringly they send new colonists into the wilderness and are building — as the Minister for Education explains — "a classroom every two hours." Ultramodern hospitals are being constructed in villages where the sick have traditionally been "cured" with Indian magic. And every day the newspapers report that the president has opened yet another stretch of road, another dam, or another factory.

Each of the presidents since Cárdenas has improved relations with the United States, believing more than ever in industrialization, and encouraging foreign investments. Land reform has taken second place to the comprehensive educational and training program on which Mexico today spends an impressive one-quarter of its national income.

In the face of such determined effort, mass poverty is receding. Alberto Lleras, ex-president of Colombia and today one of Latin America's most distinguished journalists, wrote after a visit to Mexico: "This is really a country that, in contrast to other Latin American countries, shows no signs of fatigue, no weakening of faith or of self-confidence. Here the creative and constructive spirit has suffered not at all from the stability of the political regime, which is based solely on a perfect party structure."

Lleras closes, however, with a vague apprehension that finds expression again and again: that this "perfect party structure" that has ruled Mexico for more than thirty years might strangle all interest in public affairs. By "party structure" is meant the *Partido Revolucionario Institutional*, the "party of the institutionalized revolution" that was founded by President Calles in 1929. PRI has provided all the presidents ever since. It controls both houses of parliament and, in addition, extends far beyond parliamentary representation. Most trade unions are part of the party's *Sector Obrero*, or worker's division. The PRI's influence on civil service extends from the local administration to the federal ministries; the civil servants are members of the party, integrated into its *Sector Popular*, which has over two million members. The third and largest group is still formed by the peasants, in the *Sector Campesino*. However, organized labor and government and party have developed complicated relationships.

Superficially, the PRI has the appearance of an all-embracing state party — the structure of a dictatorship. But this appearance is deceptive since all symptoms of state dictatorship are lacking in Mexico. Opposition parties, small though they be, can exist and function without hindrance. The principles of Cárdenas' socializing reforms allow the economy to retain its character of private capital; of the three hundred largest enterprises, only thirty-two are under state control. The press is free from all restrictions, apart from those that are self-imposed, and the revolution has gradually made peace even with the church. As the American Nathan L. Whetten has stated, "Individual liberty, which is enjoyed by the population in general, is the greatest benefit of the Mexican Revolution."

17 In the Capilla del Rosario at Puebla

The revolutionary party is not a petrified ideological block; quite the contrary. Precisely because the party is so comprehensive it has provided room for opposing interests. It has a monopoly, but an open one. The PRI includes radicals and liberals, members of the urban middle class and mountain peasants. It attempts to give the widely differing elements in Mexican society some common base: continuation of the revolution and promotion of social progress. Since the party functionaries are pragmatists, structure and appearance of the party change to meet the exigencies of the times.

The essential factor that preserves the party from dictatorship is the single term of the president. He is the center of influence and responsibility; in him is the culmination of power. Public life moves in its concentric circle about the president, and he is the permanent object of admiration and respect. Even Mexico cannot dispense with the strong man at its head. To keep him in check, however, the constitution limits his period of office to six years, with no possibility of reelection. *No reelección!* An iron barrier for the chief of state. As defined by American historian Frank Tannenbaum. "The man at the top must unite the whole government in his own person. He must be his own cabinet and, in this age of planning, plan his own projects. ... Everything comes within his competence. He must be able to solve all problems and find a way out of every difficulty. He must carry the full responsibility himself and a least promise to help overcome every ill ..." — but he must not seek reelection.

How Near to the United States?

"Poor Mexico, so far from God and so near to the United States." So said dictator Porfirio Díaz. In fact, Mexico had to pay dearly during the last century precisely because it lies so close to the United States. Even United States political scientist Frank R. Brandenburg found proximity to the northern colossus "extremely menacing" for Mexico.

During the most impetuous phase of American expansion, the era of "big business" and Theodore Roosevelt's "big stick," United States foreign policy was anything but delicate toward its southern neighbors. If one considers that Texas, Nevada, Utah, Arizona, part of Colorado, New Mexico, and California belonged to Mexico until 1848, then one can understand that the relations between the two countries often were highly charged with emotion. Small-scale intervention by the Americans was nothing unusual. Brandenburg cannot be contradicted when he declares that Washington saw Mexico as its "backyard." "The Central American and Caribbean countries," he writes, "suffered a painful fate whenever they forgot that anti-Americanism was a luxury that weak nations could ill-afford."

The United States had defined its relations with its neighbors south of the Rio Grande in the Monroe Doctrine, which was an attempt to deter political and military involvement by non-American nations in Latin America. Latin Americans for their part have never accepted this doctrine. It offered them no protection, but constituted the threat that the United States would enforce its own policy. Numerous landings by the U.S. Marines in the Caribbean area have demonstrated this antipathy toward the Monroe Doctrine is not without cause. In the case of Mexico, however, relations with its northern neighbor have improved considerably during the last twenty years. In September, 1964, for example, Mexico regained a tiny part of its territory that had been annexed by the Americans in 1848. This area on the Texas border, called El Chamizal by the Mexicans, covers 437.3847 acres and is of little significance in a worldwide context. But these few acres were once the theme of a seemingly endless spate of passionate Mexican oratory. Their restitution to Mexico is symptomatic of the change in Washington's attitude toward its neighbor. Mexico now works with the United States, no longer in a subservient role, but as an equal.

The Silent Indian

For several hundred years many of Mexico's Indians have succeeded in achieving an almost total geographical isolation. They live in the tiny villages in the "backwoods" that can be reached by no road, that possess no electric light. An estimated two million Mexicans, most of whom are Indians, live in villages that have fewer than a hundred inhabitants, and about eight million Mexicans, of whom most are Indians, live in villages that have fewer than five hundred people. But modern Mexico is attacking this problem of isolation with determination. It will no longer tolerate the dissociation of every fourth or fifth Mexican from the nation and the modern Mexican culture. The Indian must be promoted from his unchanged, ancient way of life into the twentieth century. New roads are each year making it possible for more Mexicains to be in closer contact with the rest of Mexico.

The geographical seclusion that naturally gives rise to a social and cultural seclusion is made even more complete by the Indian's unwillingness to abandon his ancient native language. Two million Mexican citizens cannot speak Spanish. They by no means possess a common Indian idiom, for they are isolated even from each other by about fifty-two different dialects, of which one, the Maya language in Chiapas, has as much in common with the

Aztec language of the uplands as Danish has with Russian. Very often the inhabitants of one village can hardly converse with their neighbors. Nevertheless their local linguistic tradition persists.

An hour by automobile from glittering Mexico City and its six million inhabitants it is still possible to find "backwoods" Indian villages that slumber a sleep without beginning or end, the *pueblos* without dreams. A young Mexican author, Carlos Fuentes, has described the atmosphere of the Indian village:

"A village of mud cabins that was hardly distinguishable from a thousand others. Only the *plaza* in front of the so-called town hall was paved; the other streets had a surface of dust, packed hard by the bare feet of the children, by the claws of the turkeys that preened themselves on the streets, by the paws of the pack of dogs… yapping through the village. The color of the pueblo was brown; only the facade of the town hall glinted redly. The *pueblo* lay along a river and its wealth consisted of a few turkeys and chickens, a couple of dried-out maizefields that were laid out in dirty strips, a few forges, a carpenter's shop, and a little home industry. It was a miracle how this place could exist. It existed silently."

In this village nothing has changed for half a millenium, and by our standards the Indian himself is also medieval. He is medieval as an economic being: He lives in a primitive subsistence economy that is well described by the expression *economía de centavos*, the penny economy. He plants the maize and beans that he eats, and makes his own plates and spoons. He builds the house that he lives in and weaves the matting on which he sleeps. He is his own potter and often even his own burro. For dozens of miles he trots with heavy loads in a basket on his back, the so-called Indian trap, supported by a leather thong around his forehead.

The Indian is medieval as a social being. He recognizes only the family, the clan, and the village community, which determine his behavior during the sowing and the harvest, at his birth, his baptism, his wedding, and at his death. Each village has its own folk costume, its own music and, not infrequently, its own language. But above all, each *pueblo* has its own feasts that are celebrated in honor of the village saint. Without protest the Indian submits himself to his village and his clan, which in turn exercise a form of self-government through councils of elders and wise men. Concepts such as "nation," "society," or "politics" are foreign to him.

As a religious being the Indian is even pre-medieval. He has never wholly accepted the god of the Spanish missionaries, but accords to him a certain acknowledgement nevertheless. In matters not related to family, clan, or village, his is afraid and unsure of himself. The Indians follow two religions. The saints of the Catholic Church suit them well enough, since these often can be easily identified with the pagan gods. But equally important is *el brujo*, the wizard and shaman. The shaman expedites the Indians' prayers to God, heals the sick, guarantees the harvest, fattens the family pig, and injures the enemy with magic formulas.

How deeply superstitious the Indians are can perhaps be illustrated by a story that I once heard in Guatemala, where the Maya Indians belong to the same culture as the Mayas of southern Mexico.

After the war a German immigrant was working as overseer for a construction firm building roads. He had been wounded in the war and had a glass eye, of which the Indians were much afraid. Whenever he left the work area he would remove his glass eye, put it atop a stone, then tell the Indians, "This eye will keep a watch on you and tell me later if and how you have worked." The trick worked perfectly for some time, and the Indians were more industrious under the supervision of the watching eye. But one day when the German came back he found the whole shift asleep in the shade. One of the Mayas had crept up on the eye from behind and flipped a sombrero over it as quick as lightning. Otherwise the eye would have been able to report the culprit.

The story is credible if one considers the Indians' attachment to sorcery and magic. These superstitions are centuries old, and the Indian has no intention of dissociating himself from these centuries. He wants nothing more than to plant his maize on his plot of earth and to remain true to the ways of his forefathers. A deeply-rooted mistrust separates the Indian from what he regards as the white and creole upper class, which for centuries had shamelessly exploited the indentured Indian laborers.

What then can be done to integrate the Indian into modern Mexican society? A representative of the *Instituto Nacional Indigenista*, the National Institute for Native Affairs, said: "Most Indians don't want this at all. You have no idea how hard it is to break down this wall of mistrust, fear and prejudice. The Indians have defied not only violent methods, they also attempt to elude the sincere efforts of the democratic government. Here we have to start in a very small way, right at the beginning, with education and upbringing."

The work of the National Institute for Native Affairs is governed by several principles:

To do nothing that the Indian himself does not wish and require. To do nothing that would endanger the characteristics of the Indians to such an extent that they could become a rootless urban proletariat. To not bestow charity, but to help the Indians to help themselves. Patience, enlightenment, patience.

The Institute thus begins by founding a school that becomes the nucleus of the integration process. Instructed by teachers in their own language, young and old men and women learn to read and write, learn the multiplication tables, and the Spanish language. Advisers demonstrate that building a road can increase the economic importance of a village. The Indians themselves raise rabbits and grow cabbage, bake white bread, and learn to use a sewing machine and many other tools.

Gradually the seeds of change begin to sprout. The mayor and the council of elders would like to build the road. The government sends the necessary machines and equipment, but no more. Everything else must be provided by the villagers themselves. Seeds for better types of plants and vegetables are presented free only for trials; then they must be bought by the Indians for a symbolic sum of money. "We are doing the Indian no service at all if we dull his sense of responsibility by giving him gifts." says the Institute's representative.

The most important aspect of integration is never to attempt to educate individuals. Precisely because the Indian is strongly attached to his village, this community should be the object of all educational undertakings. If the community accepts the suggestions and advice, this guarantees that all inhabitants will take part in carrying them out.

Eternal impassivity no longer has a place in modern Mexico. "With care and prudence we must get the Indians on the path of progress," explains the man from the National Institute. "We must talk to them, give them back their dignity, and raise them from the status of a second-class people. If we succeed in this the battle is won. What will then come is what we call integration of the Indian into our society and culture."

An Exploding City

He is perhaps twelve years old, the newsboy who every evening runs in and out in the turbulent traffic of Mexico City, as do hundreds of Pedros, Pablos, Juans, and Josés of the same age. He has sensationalism to offer, the stories of the big city in his evening paper. "Only forty centavos, *Señor*." For forty centavos you learn everything that keeps six million people in daily suspense. Fatal traffic accidents and film scandals. Murder provoked by jealousy. Earthquakes and affairs of corruption. Manuel, the great bullfighter. The latest lottery winner and today's horoscope. For forty centavos you get an insight into *la vida mexicana*.

That is how the newsboy would describe the contents of his paper if we asked him. A kaleidoscope of Mexico City, marketplace of sensations, flashes of the great metropolis whose rhythm and dynamic energy hold the foreigner spellbound. Described by Alexander von Humboldt as a "city of palaces," and by the Mexicans themselves as the "heart of the world," *México* is certainly one of the most beautiful cities on earth. But this beauty doesn't invite quiet observation and admiration. *México* has no time for aloofness and neutrality. This city is direct. It grabs you and holds on.

25 In the Cañon del Cobre

32   *Palace of Cortéz, Cuernavaca*

33 The Cathedral, San Miguel de Allende

México enchants with its elegance and shocks with the wretchedness of its poor. The old cliché about contrasts could actually be used for almost any city. Here, however, the contrasts clash explosively. Art and coarseness, beauty and filth, elegance and decay exist side by side. Here the skyscraper overshadows the baroque church of the Mexican colonial era. The six-lane superhighway runs alongside the mud streets of the shantytowns. The lady dressed in the latest Paris fashion walks heedlessly past the barefoot Indian woman, who squats on the sidewalk, her infant on her back, to sell peanuts. Here is the *ciudad perdida*, the lost city, separated by a concrete wall from *Lomas de Chapultepec*, the millionaires' residential district.

The Spanish invaders were dazzled by Tenochtitlán, the Aztec capital and forerunner of Mexico City, when they arrived led by Hernán Cortéz. These bold adventurers, well-traveled but used to the old continent, were particularly impressed by the order, culture and discipline of Montezuma's City of the Sun. The capital of the new Mexico, however, has lost these characteristics to a large degree. The Mexicans love their Mexico City, but even they call it "overgrown," "explosive," and "absolutely chaotic." This is understandable. Mexico City is, in fact, one of the largest cities on the North American continent and, after Buenos Aires, the largest city in Latin America. Nobody knows exactly how many people live here, crowded together, but in 1966 the number was estimated to be six million.

Three hundred thousand Aztecs were living in Tenochtitlán when the Spaniards arrived. Several years later the new rulers had reduced the number to fifty thousand. Mexico City remained a small city until the beginning of this century, when the population began a steep increase in the 1920's. Mexico City was classified as having over a million inhabitants in 1930 and by 1950 this figure had tripled. Between 1950 and 1960 another two million were added; by 1966 the figure exceeded six million. If industry, which up to now has concentrated itself in the capital and surrounding areas, doesn't discover and gradually move to the country districts, Mexico City will probably have fifteen million inhabitants by 1980. And despite the government's attempts to make the provinces more attractive, the lure of this metropolis probably will exercise its magnetism for some time to come.

A Mexican architect had a plausible explanation for this permanent invasion. "Everybody says that misery is at home in the capital. But when you consider that over three hundred thousand people come to the capital annually, then it is obvious that it isn't here, but in the country, where misery is at home."

My acquaintance explained that until the 1930's the life of a peasant was dangerous and insecure. He added, "Every Mexican has ever since been possessed by the idea that only in the capital can he enjoy a measure of security — a security based, perhaps, on the fact that here he can find a job that was denied him in the country." In fact, 62 percent of all wages earned in Mexico are paid in the Federal District, the capital. The yield here in taxes and revenues is more than from the rest of the country. Let us take a look at this country that has staked its hopes for the future on its capital.

Practically all non-Spanish-speaking foreigners, whatever their mother tongue, refer to Mexico's capital by its English name of Mexico City. Mexicans themselves usually say *México* or *De Effe*, the spoken initials at the end of the official name *México, Distrito Federal*, the equivalent of "D.C." after Washington.

And Hunger Tomorrow?

At the turn of the century Mexico had thirteen million inhabitants. The population had developed "normally," the high birthrate being offset by a high infant mortality and short life expectancy. Today life expectancy has been rapidly extended, and with the birthrate continuing to be high, Mexico has a growth rate so high that it could have 123 million inhabitants by the year 2000.

Mexico will be able to feed its enormous population only if it emerges from its present underdevelopment. And Mexico has found the way. It leads from the country into the city — not necessarily the capital — from the unprofitable small farm and self-sufficient household to participation in the diversified economic processes of a modern state. In 1930 Mexico's rural population was two-thirds of the total. In 1950, one year after the "industrial revolution" had begun, the ratio had narrowed to 57:43. The national census of 1960 showed that for the first time the towns were ahead of the country, with 51 percent. According to United Nations guidelines, Mexico will become a developed country in 1980, when two-thirds of its population will be earning their livelihood in the towns.

Certain standards for admission to the new era have been established: average income, educational level, the possession of shoes, and the consumption of wheaten bread instead of — or in addition to — the maizeflour cakes. Mexico's present standing is as follows:

Average income in the last ten years has increased considerably, to $ 320 a year (compared with $ 1,160 in West Germany, for example). However, the purchasing power of the peso has decreased by half within the same period. In 1961, 30 percent of the economically active population (about one-third of the total) still earned less than $ 35 a month, and 25 percent earned less than $ 19. Only 4 percent earned over $ 130 a month.

This last mentioned group contains the highest educational or professional level of the population, all of whom can read and write. Although among the country people the number of illiterates has decreased from 97 percent at the turn of the century to 51 percent today, there is still a tremendous difference in matters of education between urban and rural areas, and between men and women. An entrenched prejudice in rural areas against education for women has resulted in 58 percent of the rural female population remaining illiterate.

In addition to education, the town man has access to better food and clothing than does the country man. Barefooted people are not seen as frequently in Mexico City or towns, whereas 23 percent of the rural population still go through life barefoot, and 37 percent wear sandals. Only 30 percent possess shoes. Only 12 percent of the townspeople don't eat bread — or don't want to. More than 51 percent of the rural population still eat the same maize preparations that they have eaten for over a thousand years. Eighty-seven percent of the townspeople regularly consume eggs, milk, and fish, compared with 64 percent of the country people.

Only 7 percent of the Mexicans eat really well, 13 percent quite well, and 30 percent moderately well. Half of the population is definitely underfed. Forty percent can seldom afford anything better than maize and black beans, and 10 percent must ultimately be satisfied with a single, insufficient meal per day. This last group belongs to that fifth of the Latin American population that must exist on less than a thousand calories per day. This diet borders on brutal hunger. The minimum daily ration even in postwar Germany during the worst years contained at least 1350 calories per day.

A combination of malnutrition and explosive population growth is hardly one to inspire hope for the future. Nevertheless not all the experts are pessimistic. Some think Mexico will be capable of feeding 123 million people by the year 2000 if the land reform program replaces small farms with larger production units. Although only 14 percent of Mexico's land area is arable, settlement and cultivation will be increased greatly. Irrigation, mechanization, better agricultural methods, and a wider range of crops can multiply agricultural yields.

To this end, however, schooling and instruction are a necessary addition to credit. Some Indian peasants are still indifferent to "economic" thinking or even planning. The Indian often works only as many days as are necessary for him to survive and to indulge in the few local celebrations; seventy working days are sufficient for the Maya. He can't demand anything when nobody and nothing stimulates him. The Indian is now about to receive a gentle shove from the government, because it is no longer just a question of his personal survival alone. It concerns the future of a hundred million Mexicans.

Despite this unpromising picture, it is generally anticipated that this hundred million will have more and better food to eat than their fathers and grandfathers, although a competent judge of the situation, the president of Mexico's Chamber of Commerce, E. Escandon, has declared that land reform "has by and large been a failure." It will be more difficult to provide the growing population with the bare necessities of life and with a living standard that is already taken for granted in Europe and the United States. The avalanche of births has to be channeled annually into 400,000 new jobs, and that means industrialization, accelerated and rapid industrialization.

The birth pangs and teething troubles of this process are already past. Industry is growing so vigorously that Mexico can truly be called "the Japan of Latin America." Today industry contributes the largest part of the gross national product, and is upholding its responsibility to the population increase. Mexico now shares with Brazil, Argentina, and Chile the reputation of being the most economically stable countries south of the United States. Except for Chile, Mexico is politically far ahead of its nearest competitors. The reasons? The revolution has been reoriented toward continuous progress, and the military is dedicated to the preservation of national security. The foundation is healthier, the currency hard and freely convertible, the inflow of capital enormous, and the outflow by no means catastrophic.

Precious metals first made Mexico economically attractive to Europe. The country was conquered during the fifteenth-century goldrush. The conquistadores wanted to make themselves and the Spanish crown rich as quickly as possible with the legendary golden treasures of the Aztecs and Mayas. Above all things, gold inspired the ruthless plundering expeditions of the conquistadores, and they found gold. But they found even more silver. Up to the present day Mexico has remained the most important silver-producing country in the world. The silver city of Taxco glitters with "the white ordure of the gods," artistically worked and molded by the silversmiths in breathtaking quantities. Here in Taxco stands the home of José de la Borda, who in the eighteenth century was reckoned to be the "richest man under the Earth's surface." He could have paved his patio with silver, and according to legend, actually did.

Silver was responsible for both legend and history. In 1900 eighty percent of Mexico's income from exports came from minerals, but today mining has lost this preeminence, and the decline seems to be continuing. However, Mexico ranks as the world's third greatest producer of lead, fourth in the production of zinc and sulfur, ninth in copper, and tenth in gold. The deposits of manganese are so large that the needs of the steel industry can be met for many years to come. For the time being, domestic iron ore supplies the steel industry, and with the discovery of new coal fields, Mexico can now claim first place in Latin America in steel production.

Mexico, like Texas, floats on a black sea. The Mexican cornucopia gushes oil that has affected not only the economy but often the politics of the country, and particularly its international relations. The extraction of Mexican oil was exclusively in American and European hands until President Cárdenas caused a crisis with the United States and Great Britain in 1938 by nationalizing the oil fields and their equipment. Today the oil monopoly is controlled by the state-owned PEMEX, which administers Latin America's second largest oil deposits after Venezuela. In this connection the other economic sectors might be mentioned in which the influence of foreign capital is likewise not tolerated in the petroleum and chemical industries, electricity supply, transport and electrical rail service, railroads, credit institutions, and insurance companies. In these branches the Mexicans are strictly *"mexicanissimo."*

In Teotihuacán and Tula it is history written in stone that fascinates the visitor. In the Indian villages of Oaxaca and Michoacán, the country's past reaches into the present. In Mexico City and Monterrey, however, it is the future that greets the visitor's eye. There, Mexican industry has created imposing production complexes: Monterrey as the center of heavy industry and the Federal District of Mexico as the production center of consumer goods. Today Mexico has over a hundred thousand manufacturing companies. According to the volume of their production, they rank as follows: foodstuffs and beverages (Mexico is self-sufficient, and its beer production, for example, is the tenth largest in the world), textiles, iron and steel, tobacco, paper and soap, and cement, which has undergone particularly rapid expansion.

When a country industrializes suddenly, it often creates "prestige" enterprises, supporting these industries with high protective duty or total import embargo. This "super protection" not only tends to create monopolies, it all but excludes competition. The result is often poorly-made but expensive products. Mexico was spared this development through the high incidence of foreign capital investments.

Imports, assembly works, and construction under license predominate in the motor vehicle industry. Volkswagen, for example, has developed into the largest motor vehicle producer in Mexico. The automobile firm from Wolfsburg, Germany, has established an extensive plant in Puebla, a remarkable achievement in the face of strong American competition. Such a large project naturally promotes development in steel, rubber, electrical and metalworking industries, all of which have grown considerably in the last few years.

Daring Projects and Abject Misery

Many newcomers to the capital are paupers, arriving barefoot from some impoverished province to seek their fortune in the big city. They settle on the periphery of the town in dwellings that are hardly fit for human habitation. Their hovels of planks, cardboard, and corrugated iron are perhaps little worse than the mud cabins they occupied at home, but here at least they live in the glare of city lights where Fortune, in a lax moment, may be wooed and won.

Not all capture Fortune's favor. A newspaper announced in the summer of 1965 that in the *Barranca del Muerto,* the Ravine of Death, countless families still live in caves and holes in the ground without any sanitary facilities. "The place is somewhat worse than a rubbish dump. It is a cesspool. Tens of thousands of families live here like rats, moles or other vermin. Their promiscuity and lack of hygiene give rise to illness, hatred and crime."

American anthropologist Oscar Lewis has presented an example of this great city's poverty, an account which has caused a sensation even in Europe. Lewis made friends with the Sanchez family, who lived in a gigantic tenement block and who recounted their life-history into a tape recorder over a period of several years. The family is entrapped in an environment that Oscar Lewis defines as the culture of poverty. According to the anthropologist, members of this culture have the following distinguishing characteristics:

Their educational level is below normal. They belong to neither trade unions nor political parties, and display little interest in things or events outside their four walls. They spend less time than other people in banks, hospitals, museums, churches, and shops. They live a hand-to-mouth existence and generally purchase used furniture and clothes. They do the unskilled jobs, suffer most from unemployment and low wages, generally live in overcrowded living quarters, are inclined to settle personal conflicts with violence, and to treat women and children with brutality. Early sexual experience, loose marital unions, and a higher frequency of divorce are symptoms of the culture of poverty.

Mexico City is not, of course, the only town with a slum. Guadalajara, Monterrey, Chihuahua, Puebla, and Veracruz all have their shantytowns, and indeed all Latin American cities are encircled by these breeding grounds of vice and political unrest. A case in point is the *favellas* of Rio de Janeiro, depicted in the film "Black Orpheus." The Mexican government, however, is carrying out an energetic slum clearance program. Between 1958 and 1964, during President Adolfo Lopez Mateos' term of office, 86 miles of new water mains and 253 miles of new drains were laid, 21 miles of new city highways were built, along with 26 city kindergartens, 170 schools, 88 shopping centers, 10 sports grounds, 17 general hospitals, 2 children's hospitals, and 1,008 acres of new parks and green areas.

The government is increasing the number of dwelling units through bold construction projects. An enormous slum district, for example, was razed, and at a cost of one billion pesos the government is building apartments for 70,000 people — with schools, self-service shops, sports grounds and children's playgrounds, cinemas, and parks. Everywhere apartment blocks and rows of houses are rising between the shantytowns; everywhere stand the complexes of the *Seguro Social,* the social security organization, which is attempting to eradicate the worst forms of misery in Mexico. Ultramodern and well-equipped hospitals stand beside social assistance offices, maternal counseling centers, and special children's aid bureaus.

It is more than material privation that the Mexicans are seeking to do away with through these projects. As they remove the blemishes from their city's face, they are also trying to overcome the psychological distress. The new Mexico is striving to encourage a scientific, technical, and economical pragmatism to replace apathy among the citizenry and authoritarianism in government. And where should this pragmatism have its roots if not at the universities and colleges?

Mexico's national university, *Universidad Nacional,* is a marvel of modern architecture. It is not just a university in the traditional European sense. It is a city of the sciences, with 72,000 students whose study costs them practically nothing. Like the grade-school and high-school pupils and those adults who are just learning to read and write, the university students are part of the education budget to which Mexico allots a quarter of its national income. In contrast to this, 10 percent is devoted to the military budget, which is extremely low by Latin American standards. But most important of all, the university is a cornerstone of Mexican pride — it is the materialization of a unique heritage, of Mexicanism.

The national university gives perhaps the most impressive picture of the new Mexico. However, in the capital, one finds the beauty of old Mexico in all shades and variations.

Five cultures are to be discovered in Mexico City. Least evident is probably the original Aztec culture, since Tenochtitlán was completely razed by Cortéz. From the stones of the Aztec temple the Spaniards built the cathedral, the largest in Latin America, and the administration buildings around the main square, the *Zócalo,* which is the heart and center of the city. The narrow streets, the churches, arcades, convents, and patios behind the *Zócalo* faithfully reflect late medieval Spanish towns. The spectacular *Paseo de la Reforma,* which was laid out by the Emperor Maximilian, is copied after the *Champs-Elysées.* After the revolution Mexico became more Mexican in its architecture, but now the garish influence of the big neighbor is making itself felt and illuminated advertisements and neon signs stretch as far as the eye can see.

And the eye can see far indeed when one is standing on top of the *Torre Latinoamericana:* It is Latin American Tower, a forty-three story skyscraper, with a restaurant on the top floor, and with dozens of offices, many of which are rented to lawyers. The presence of the lawyers might be explained by the fact that Mexico is one Mecca for would-be divorcees.

The *Torre* lies at the junction of two main thoroughfares, over whose six asphalt lanes an endless stream of traffic comes and goes. From the tower one sees the colossal marble *Bellas Artes.* Inside, its massive dimensions seem to vaporize when the lights are dimmed in the auditorium for performances of Mexico's *Ballet Folklorico,* which enchants both locals and visitors. Beside the ponderous and majestic *Bellas Artes* lies Alameda Park, dominated by the monument to Benito Juárez, the father of modern Mexico. This greenery in the middle of the city is plainly a people's haven. Whole families come here to picnic, lovers hold hands, and children roll in the grass. Shoeshine boys, ice-cream vendors, fruit-juice and fruit hawkers, newsboys, lottery-ticket sellers, and balloon vendors do business where the Inquisition pursued its sinister occupation 150 years ago. The park photographer puts his head beneath his black cloth and records for posterity the historic first visit of a large country familiy to the capital. A group of schoolgirls in freshly starched uniforms pay their reverent respects to the stone Juárez while the tourists roam with cameras at the ready — standing, kneeling, lying — to shoot what comes into their lenses.

Seen from the battlements of the *Torre,* the skyline of Mexico's Manhattan scrawls the stony signature of a new era across the pale-blue sky that arches serene and unmoved over splendor and misery alike. The Square of the Three Cultures forms the bridge between yesterday and tomorrow. Around the ruined Aztec temple, the sixteenth-century church, and the twenty-first-century Polytechnical Institute is grouped the satellite city of Nonoalco, the great architectural feat of modern Mexico. The castle of Chapultepec, once a residence of Maximilian and of the republican Porfirio Díaz, rises out of the green carpet of Chapultepec Park, looking provincial, like the family seat of an impoverished European princeling. The University City is barely visible on the far side of this panorama. Out of sight lies the millionaires' "dream city," Pedregal, a city of glass, concrete, and lava, more daring in execution than all the visions of an architects' congress. Pedregal is cut off from its unkempt surroundings by a sort of Berlin Wall, which can, however, be penetrated through several iron gates. The millionaires have shut themselves behind a wall. What admirable arrogance!

Mexico City is undoubtedly one of the world's most beautiful cities. Although new superlatives are being created daily, the skyscraper is a real miracle of statics and mathematics. During its construction two factors had to be taken into consideration: the swampy ground and the earthquakes.

When Cortéz arrived at Tenochtitlán the city was girded by lakes and bayous. The Spaniards filled in many of the canals with rubble from Montezuma's City of the Sun, but the capital of the Viceroy of New Spain could still claim to be the "Venice of the New World." It was, nevertheless, a pestilential "Venice." Epidemics and Spanish negligence transformed the lakes into breeding grounds of bacteria, and the Spaniards, perhaps with the bone-dry Castilian landscape in mind, single-mindedly attempted to be rid of them no matter what the cost. A German immigrant sold them the ingenious idea of boring a tunnel through one of the surrounding mountains to let the water run off. The tunnel was bored and the water drained away, but instead of settling onto a solid base, the city sank onto a bed of soft mud.

As long as Mexico City remained a small town, the condition of the building sites was of little importance; the "sponge" on which Mexico City stood swelled with water during the rainy season and was able to support the city. With the rapid growth of the capital, however, the pressure of masses of stone and concrete increased enormously. Moreover, the asphalting of streets prevented rainwater from soaking into the substrata, which in turn is continually being pumped out to meet the needs of increasing water consumption. The sponge dried up and shrank.

As a result, the city annually subsides twelve to sixteen inches into swampy ground, with the larger and heavier buildings naturally sinking more quickly than the smaller and lighter ones, thus creating grotesque street fronts. A two-story apartment house hangs, displaced and distorted, between two attractive bank buildings. Not only the apartment house but the sidewalk in front of the banks has been dragged down by the heavy buildings. Even in the center of the city one sometimes gets the impression that one is driving over a plowed field. Pedestrians also have their problems since the curb of the sidewalk is often knee-high above the street surface.

To circumvent the whims of the waterlogged subsoil, the previous generation of architects constructed their buildings on pilings driven down to the solid stone layer beneath the morass. Now, while the rest of the city is subsiding with beautiful regularity, the buildings on pilings are growing out of the ground — at the same rate as the city is sinking. It has become necessary every year to add a few new steps to the Angel of Liberty monument on the *Paseo de la Reforma*. The Republic Memorial, which was also built on pilings, now stands on top of a hill, although it was originally erected on level ground.

A different construction principle was used with the Latin American Tower to make the building earthquake-proof and solve the problem of subsidence. The giant stands on enormous buoyant tanks that move effortlessly with the overall motion of the city. During one of the strongest earthquakes of the last few years not a single window in the building even cracked, although roofs, walls, and whole houses collapsed in the neighborhood.

The cracks on most of the house fronts are caused less by general settling of the city than by earth tremors traceable to the two volcanoes, Popocatépetl and Ixtacihuatl. The visitor will at first admire the beautiful, snow-covered backdrop on the horizon, but anyone who has been thrown out of bed by the volcanoes' convulsions — as once happened to me — would gladly relinquish the decorative scenery. Nevertheless, the people live in the volcanoes' shadow.

Who are the six million people who crowd together in the capital? And what sort of people are they? The writer Rosales says:

"The people of the capital are cosmopolitan. Here contact with the unfamiliar takes place, accompanied by a broadening of the mind. Even the children of the capital possess a certain boldness which they breathe in with the city air. They are more mature and aware than the country children. The youth is more eager and better educated because better opportunities exist here. The women are more sophisticated and versatile. To be a citizen of the capital is to have climbed one more step up from mediocrity."

But the transformation can only take place slowly and painfully. An American sociologist has said that "Mexico's political stability is nothing more than evidence of the Mexican's ability to endure brutal poverty and suffering." These resilient people are easy to find in Mexico City. The street is their parliament, their work place and trading post, sometimes even their dormitory, and nearly always their dining place. It was precisely these men of the streets that the Brazilian author Erico Verissimo had in mind:

"In Mexico I saw the people. In the United States, a country that consists almost exclusively of the middle class, one never sees the people. There one sees only individuals, who meet each other by chance or who, as members of the same club, collect around a table in a disciplined group to eat, to listen or to make speeches. The people — that is Mexico."

The people that inhabit the slums of Mexico, however, are just as isolated from their surroundings as the millionaires behind their wall in Pedregal. A slum lives by its own laws, and all too often by its own lawlessness. Just as in the slums of most large cities, several people daily die a violent death. Some apologists are quick to offer explanations for the violence and harshness, equating it with virility exemplified with the Mexican *machismo*.

Mexico today is, however, populated for the most part by *mestizos,* the descendants of whites and Indians. The *mestizo* has gone down in history as the racial bridge between white and red. With him the union between Europe and American was created. No longer an Indian, yet not a white man, in the social hierarchy of the colonial era his place was on the second level from the bottom. In contrast to the closely knit groups above and below, he had no deep roots or firm traditional stand. The *mestizo* could not sink any lower, since the Indians no longer accepted him.

As a civilized person one should wish to avoid generalizations or making conclusions on the basis of some racial theory, but even the Mexicans regard themselves as *raza nueva,* a new race. A memorial tablet on the Square of the Three Cultures in Nonoalco commemorates the birth of the *raza mestiza,* the *mestizo* race, and a well-known writer has even extolled his compatriots as *raza cósmica,* a cosmic race. These citations alone are enough to show that Mexico knows no racial prejudices. On the contrary, the Indian is today romanticized, sometimes to the detriment of the white man as personified by the Spaniard.

This sociological starting point can perhaps explain why politics became the favorite occupation of the ambitious *mestizo,* since it was the quickest and surest way to prestige, power, and wealth. A degree of distrust and xenophobia, apparent to the foreigner in the capital, serve as protection and safeguard against the intruder. They are part of the Indian heritage, motivated and validated by hundreds of precedents. The traces of subjugation cannot be eradicated in the twinkling of an eye.

The visitor to Mexico City will find its Janus visage won't leave him indifferent. *"Como México no hay dos."*

Piety in a Secular State

Good Friday in Taxco. The city breaks into religious ecstasy. A procession of penitents moves slowly through the steep and narrow streets of the silver city. Women in black cowls and hoods crawl laboriously over the cobbles, dragging chains behind them. Blood streams from torn knees. Men, stripped to the waist, carry bundles of thorns as big as tree trunks across their necks. Others scourge their backs with barbed whips until the blood spurts from the flayed skin.

Muffled chorales resound from the cathedral to be repeated by the panting penitents on the street. The Indians have come to Taxco in thousands from the surrounding villages. Each village carries its own statue of the Savior in the procession, and the heavy Indian faces reflect every phase of Christ's passion. If the suffering of Christ be imitated and expiated on Good Friday anywhere in the world, it is here on the cobblestones of the Mexican silver city, Taxco. This is no tourist spectacle, but piety.

There can be no question that as a people the Mexicans are pious. But — and this seems to be a paradox — they are not Catholic, except superficially. It is true that 93 percent of all Mexicans are baptized in the Catholic Church, but this figure proves little, if anything. Most

Mexicans accepted with indifference the bloody persecution of the Catholic Church by the state at the end of the 1920's and the constitution that placed unprecedented limitations on the Catholic Church. They have been equally indifferent, in recent decades, to the government's lax enforcement of these same constitutional limitations. The Mexican Indians' conversion was not exactly characterized by priestly gentleness on the part of the Spanish missionaries who followed Hernán Cortéz and the conquistadores. But it was probably less the harshness of the missions than the Indians' attachment to the old magical cults that impeded the propagation and acceptance of the Roman Catholic faith. The Indians allowed themselves to be baptized, and learned to pray the "Our Father" and to cross themselves. But they then superimposed the new religion to a certain extent on their old rituals, assimilated their old gods, and turned Catholicism into a cult where almost every saint has his pagan counterpart. It is still probable that most Mexican Catholics know nothing, and want to know nothing, about Roman Catholic dogma. Tenets of the faith, such as the Trinity, the Incarnation, or the infallibility of the Pope are unknown and immaterial to them, nor do they orient themselves by Rome. Often enough Christ himself must take second place to some village saint. The national "Virgin of Guadalupe, the Patroness of America" always is ranked before the Virgin Mary, and for Mexico, Central America, and much of South America the *Virgen Morena*, the dark or brown virgin, is the highest religious authority, although her origin and legend are enveloped in mystery.

Legend has it that the Virgin appeared for the first time in the darkness on the ninth of December, 1531, to the Indian Juan Diego. She called herself the mother of God and the mother of all Indians. And she sent Juan Diego, so he said, to Bishop Zumarraga with the request that he build her a chapel at the spot where she had appeared. Even this place, however, had its pagan background: before the arrival of the Spaniards the temple of the Aztec mother god Tonantzin had stood there. Bishop Zumarraga hesitated, but Juan Diego reported that the dark virgin appeared a second and a third time. As a sign of her godly mission, she made roses grow on a stony field, telling the Indian to take them to the doubting bishop. As Juan Diego unfolded his cloak before the churchly dignitary to shake out the roses, he found that they had vanished. In their place was the image of the brown madonna,

34 *Stone Figures at the Temple of Tula*

88

which today hangs above the altar in the Basílica of Tepeaca, the most precious relic of all Indian Catholics.

Objections and protests were raised against the story of the miracle again and again through the centuries, and Rome never elevated the belief in the "Patroness of America" to the rank of a dogma. This, however, didn't disturb the Indians and *mestizos* in the slightest. For them the dark virgin was and remains the incarnation of Catholicism. It was her picture that the rebels under the excommunicated priest Hidalgo carried on their flags. It was in her name that Mexico was liberated. The reverence accorded her by the people is so deeply ingrained and so fervent that it is as impossible to dispel her from the faith of Mexico's lower classes as it would be to exclude Christ from the churches of Christendom. Her image is in many houses, in many drinking halls, in many buses, and on her feast day, December 12, the pilgrims stream from every corner of Mexico to the Basílica of Tepeaca. Octavio Paz describes the atmosphere of this most important of all the countless holy days: "There are certain days on which the entire country, from the remotest village to the greatest cities, prays, celebrates, howls, gets drunk, and commits suicide, all in honor of Benito Juárez or the Virgin of Guadalupe." Whoever has experienced the twelfth of December in Tepeaca, or who has only read the police reports of the day's occurrences, will certainly not contradict Octavio Paz.

The higher clergy and the upper classes always remained aloof from the disreputable religious exuberance of the masses. They had nothing but contempt for the Black Madonna; but they were intelligent enough not to banish her to the regions of superstition. In this way they retained the people, at least nominally, for Catholicism, although the unadulterated Roman Catholic teachings became more and more a class religion. The "purity" of the belief decreases with every step down the social scale.

The practice of the faith, however, depends not only on social position but also on the sex of the person — even on geography. In areas where many European immigrants settled, and which have retained their Spanish traditions, the people are more active in a religious sense. Everywhere the woman is more intense in her faith than the man. She seeks from the parish priest what is denied her by her husband in his masculine self-confidence: advice, consolation, comfort, understanding. For the man, the religious crisis usually begins with puberty. His upbringing, his surroundings, and his models of behavior force the young man to an immoderate virility that forbids him to humble himself even in religion. In the opinion of the sociologists, this exaggerated masculinity — the notorious *machismo* — is also responsible for the serious and permanent crisis in Mexican Catholicism.

The men of the lower classes are particularly susceptible to *machismo*. Their speech alone is a massive blasphemy, and religious feeling is conspicuously lacking — apart from a stealthy devotion to the Virgin of Guadalupe. In the middle and upper-middle classes the percentage of practicing Catholics increases; but the strength of the prerevolutionary landowning upper class, once the main pillar of Mexican Catholicism, has been all but eliminated.

The revolution of 1910 dramaticized the already tense relationship between church and state. It took an uncompromising stand against the Catholicism of the Spanish bishops who, on their side, formed an equally uncompromising front against the political and social upheaval. In four main areas church and state have clashed since Mexico's independence: ownership of church property, child rearing and education, clerical intervention in politics, and the number and nationality of the priests.

The property owned by the Mexican church toward the end of the colonial era was excessive. The church's income was higher than that of the state; over half of the land and the immovable capital was in the hands of the clergy, which had succeeded in obtaining inordinate privileges for itself. Mexico was all but carpeted with monasteries and churches — the little town of Cholula, for example, could honor the 365 saints of the year separately in 365 churches.

The immense possessions of the church were by no means divided evenly among the clergy. The estates were almost without exception the personal property of the bishops. Even the deeply religious Carlotta, consort of the interim Emperor Maximilian, was unable to suppress her indignation when she wrote to a European friend that "village priests are dying of hunger while the bishops are living amidst indescribable luxury and abundance." The misery of the country people never again was mentioned. It was the will of God, and was endured with a dull lethargy until the revolution of 1910.

Even before the revolution, however, the position of the church as a leading economic power was progressively undermined, the first presidents having begun the secularization of the church property. Nevertheless, one third of the cultivated land still belonged to the church when the liberal President Benito Juárez nationalized all church estates in 1857 and forbade the church to acquire property or lend money for interest. The revolution further increased the state's anticlerical activity, and exceeded the liberals of the nineteenth century by passing a law that made all completed church buildings the property of the state. Small wonder that Mexico City, for example, is full of half-built churches in which Masses are celebrated nevertheless.

The church's monopoly in education and upbringing was also a challenge to be answered by state intervention. The church schools were too Spanish and exclusive, and 90 percent of Mexico's population were illiterate. In the turbulent early years of the revolution even the few existing schools were closed and the last clerical teachers expelled. President Cárdenas placed the educational system on a completely new footing in 1934 when he introduced the public, so-called "socialist schools." The clergy protested against the "atheist schools," but their influence was waning. The church was becoming more compliant and thoughtful by the middle of the 1930's, as the clergy realized that they could not successfully oppose the state. Although private Catholic schools were gradually permitted to reopen, the church was simply not capable of carrying out a program of mass education.

The bishops were used to influencing the politics of the country directly; for example, they had refused the sacraments to all officials taking an oath under Benito Juárez' 1857 constitution. With one move the revolutionary constitutionalists had done away with the church's direct political influence. Priests were forbidden to criticize Mexican laws and governmental organization, and they were deprived of voting rights. Political parties with Christian titles were forbidden.

Under President Calles the anticlerical laws took arbitrary forms. Calles forbade all open-air processions, and priests were not allowed to appear in public in soutanes or in Mass vestments. Inspired by Calles, a "Catholic National Church" was founded and freemasonry and Protestantism were encouraged. The hardest blow to the church, however, was the government's decision that individual states should determine the number of priests "according to the religious need." In 1931 the entire state of Tabasco found "no religious need"; therefore, no priests were allowed in. The church struck back against this suppression. All Mexican churches were closed by the clergy, who refused to administer the sacraments. They called for a mass revolt against the "atheist" constitution in general and against Calles in particular. Small insurrections broke out in several parts of the country, but they were suppressed by President Calles not without cruelty and bloodshed. This rebellion of the *cristeros* was the last organized resistance to the revolution.

The church now had to suffer the consequenzes of its indifferent stewardship during its period of establishment in the old colony: it had never seriously nurtured Catholicism as a religion of the people. Now the millions of peasants were certainly not going to man the barricades simply because a priest — probably a Spaniard — ordered them to. They were so estranged from the Roman Church that they remained immovable as long as the Black Madonna or their village saints were not threatened. They understood nothing of the quarrels between the higher clergy and the state.

When Calles had driven out the Spanish priests and bishops and ordained that only Mexicans by birth could be ministers of a "religious cult,", the church became exclusively Mexican for the first time. It underwent a profound structural change, discarded the feudalistic garb of medieval, royalist, and Spanish-oriented Catholicism, and became more democratic. To the degree that the church "mexicanized" itself and accorded the state a certain loyalty, the relationship between the antagonists relaxed. With the sensational avowal of President Avila Camacho, *"Yo soy creyente,"* I am a believer, the "atheism" of the revolutionary state lost its asperity.

Today the undeclared truce has developed into peaceful coexistence, and the church can exercise a degree of influence. A reconciliation with the Vatican that it also in the wind hints at a resumption of diplomatic relations broken by the Holy See because of Benito Juárez' anticlerical laws. It is indeed remarkable that one of the countries exhibiting the most symbols and forms of Catholicism should not be officially represented at the Vatican.

Woman and Maidservant

The Indian is continually on the move. The processions hurry along the highways and footpaths on the way to market or public festival, and the order of march is always the same. In front trots the man and five paces behind him his wife, generally more heavily laden than he. Even on the city sidewalks the Indian woman keeps at an appropriate distance behind him. She squats at his feet while he takes his ease on a park bench in the plaza. This aloofness alone is enough to indicate the gulf between the sexes. Traditionally this woman has been relegated to a position of inferiority. She rules over pots, pans, and children; the man rules over everything else.

The arrival of the Spaniards increased the dependence of the woman. The Moorish seraglio mentality of the Andalusians joined in a dubious alliance with the Indian conception, which required of the woman not partnership but self-sacrifice. For centuries the Mexican woman was a creature that accepted its destiny with patience and submission. In his treatise on the "Personality of the Mexican Woman," Miguel Loreto discusses several characteristics of her role in the home. She is described as kind, obedient to the point of self-denial, long-suffering, even holy and a martyr, but never as being efficient and energetic. These compliments are reserved for the man, whose individuality and manliness beget the extremes of *machismo*.

Loreto's explanations of the enormous difference between the sexes in Mexico are more academic than historical. The separate behavior patterns for boys and girls are fixed by the parents at home. The boy is initiated early by the father into the hard rules of life as laid down by the struggle for existence in Mexico. In contrast, the girl's upbringing is directed exclusively toward marriage and domestic life. Loreto's observations, still valid for broad sections of the Mexican population, give a clear and true picture of the situation thirty years ago when women did not possess the right to vote (they received it in 1958), could not occupy public office, and were not even allowed to appear as witnesses in court. Without the consent of her husband a woman could neither travel nor obtain a passport. The acquisition of property was forbidden to her, she was not allowed to manage her own inheritance or dowry, or dispose of it, and unmarried women had to remain with their parents until they were least thirty years old. "This distinctive masculine world," said the Latin American magazine *Vision* in the autumn of 1964, "has vanished once and for all."

The magazine's bright vision is true, however, only for the larger cities and the capital. Here the woman has taken over ministerial and administrative posts, diplomatic missions, and parliamentary seats. She not only works in offices and stores, she also operates computers and plans economic projects. The statistics proudly point to the 300 women lawyers currently practicing in Mexico, as compared with one in 1927. Forty-six women architects and twenty-five women engineers have established themselves in professions which were open only to men twenty-five years ago. Twelve percent of the medical profession is recruited from among women. And a woman sits at the steering wheel of every fifth automobile.

These figures are very modest by European or American standards. Just the same, a beginning has been made, and a sphere once limited to children, kitchen, and church is weakening. The number of working women is increasing from day to day; already one in every four university students is a woman. This development is indeed revolutionary when one realizes that for centuries it was considered indecent for a woman to have any education whatever. The reluctance of the rural people, particularly the Indians, to send girls to school is the last evidence of this attitude. Here it is still the tradition that a woman may only leave the house to go to Mass.

As has already been mentioned, Mexico is shaping itself more and more after the urban models of industrial society. Women constitute 20 percent of the working force, but this statistic is deceptive. One occupation requiring neither training nor education outstrips all others by a ratio of ten to one. The maidservant, *criada, sirvienta,* or *muchacha,* doesn't need to know very much. In popular parlance, the maidservants are called *gatas,* cats, because their sleeping quarters are generally in the attics of the apartment houses.

It is estimated that as many maidservants are working in Mexico City alone as there are people in the state of Vermont, about 400,000. For every fifteen people there is one *muchacha,* a ratio which proves that a maidservant is not a luxury. When a family has climbed the first step up from poverty, the first thing it does is provide itself with a *muchacha,* and many families employ three or four of these girls, each of whom has her own special job to do: cooking, cleaning, washing, ironing, or taking care of the children. For the *patrón,* the number of maidservants is a status symbol; the more numerous the servants, the greater the prestige.

Twenty-six dollars a month is considered to be top wages for a *muchacha,* and social security contributions have not yet been introduced. Nevertheless, to a girl who has been working on a farm for 25 cents a day the big city offers attractive wages. The *muchacha* even has her own room, relatively good food, and so much money that her family at home in one of the impoverished provinces can enjoy a higher standard of living. The fascination of the metropolis is understandable.

Many young girls, however, exchange the poverty-stricken security of the country much too quickly for the glittering misery of the big town. Hardly are they settled in Mexico City when they take a *novio,* a fiancé. Then they must marry or live with a seventeen-year-old lover. About half of the Mexican marriages consist of such loose liaisons which also produce 40 percent of the children. When the number of the children gets too large — and it gets large perforce, since the only way the man can demonstrate his *machismo* is by a large family — the difficulty of providing the daily bread becomes insurmountable, and many men desert their commonlaw families to look for a new "fiancée." An inquiry has shown that 12 percent of the maidservants in Mexico City are abandoned mothers.

The fate of these girls provides a far more accurate measure of the status of Mexican women than does the count of a few dozen female engineers, architects, or editors. But even here change is making itself felt, and the time is drawing near when the terms "woman" and "maidservant" will no longer be synonymous.

Papageno, Goldmouth, and Other Goblins

This capital, Mexico City, is surely the focus of all the country's uproar. From morning until night horns blow and bells ring, men and boys whistle, shout, and sing, musicians play, and radios blare. Every action is accompanied by a special background that tells those in the know what is going on. They hear signals among sounds that are as yet undifferentiated for the foreigner. He has no idea what it means when someone on the street whistles or shouts; but gradually he learns. It means that the ministering house goblins are there, each announcing his appearance with a particular hullabaloo.

A long, drawn-out, raucous proclamation rends the air. Aha! The garbage man in a peaked cap and overalls is pulling a little wooden cart on iron wheels, on which sits an empty tar barrel. The servant girls carry out the garbage cans, and gradually the barrel fills with the rubbish of a great city. The *basurero*, the garbage man, is an important figure in Mexico City. He normally works accompanied by a *pepenador*, who immediately forages among the latest contents of the garbage barrel. The *pepenador* is one rank beneath tha *basurero*, and it is typical of the Mexicans' macabre sense of humor that they call death *"el pepenador"* — garbage carrier, scavenger, rag dealer. The *pepenador* gets no wages for his work, subsisting

44 *The Monastery Church of Santo Domingo, Oaxaca*

On the Beach at Cozumel

from his finds; but the *basurero*, on the other hand, collects 25 cents per week from each family whose rubbish he carts away. For this sum he bellows his arrival daily except on Sunday.

On the heels of private enterprise follows the city-operated garbage service which costs nothing but is also not quite reliable. Like the old-time village crier, the garbage man swings his bell. His shouts and cries can be heard streets away, and are the impatiently awaited sign for the servant girls to gather and gossip on the street corner. The milk boy has no need of a mechanical amplifier. Between his fingers he blasts a whistle that would melt the shell of a century-old tortoise. With the melodious triple tones of a rococo carillon, the iceman daintily tries to tempt customers. The balloon seller plays a nasal wooden whistle, while wonderfully lyric chords from a sort of organ flute announce the man who offers hot chestnuts out of a gaily colored little locomotive. The barrel-organ player collects copper coins in return for the old revolutionary song, "*La cucaracha*" — the sad ballad about the cockroach that could no longer walk or run about, because it had no marihuana.

On the corner the fruit dealer is now visible and audible, offering for sale his basketful of fruit, a veritable tropical cornucopia. A long, drawn-out "*flooorees*" heralds the flower seller. Now a heavy truck honks up the street. Two men climb out to unload twenty-quart bottles and carry them into the houses. These are the water carriers delivering *agua puro*, purified and bacteria-free water that you can even drink. Though every Mexican will assure the visitor that water from city mains is purer and more delicious than the water of medicinal springs, the vendors do a thriving business.

Now we hear the four-toned panpipes with which Papageno also announces himself in Mozart's opera, "The Magic Flute." It isn't Papageno, but the postman, and after him the scissors-sharpener with the same signal. An old Indian woman scurrying from house to house barefooted and almost invisible under her shawl has no need to proclaim her wares. All doors are open to the *tortillera*, who bakes and sells Mexico's favorite food, the *tortilla*, a flat cake of maize flour. The Mexicans eat *tortillas* with every meal.

A distinctive ministering goblin now stands at the door and demands tribute. It is the auxiliary policeman who defends us at night from miscreants and robbers, receiving for this service about 13 cents a week. He assures us, it is true, that this payment is voluntary, but the man is of such frightening mien that we would not risk losing his protection. The auxiliary policeman doesn't shout, probably because he isn't able to. His whole mouth is full of gold teeth — a complete set of dentures — without a single white gap. His jaws are as full of gold pegs as his belt is full of cartridges. We call our guardian goblin "Goldmouth" and his mustachioed companion, elegantly swinging a rubber truncheon as he watches the financial transaction, "Narcissus."

Then come the "gas men" who in Mexico replace the city gas works common to other countries. Here every householder has to provide his own supply, so gas cylinders are always to be seen in backyards or on roofs of houses. They are delivered on order so that the flame of the gas stove doesn't go out. But of course it goes out anyway, almost with the regularity of sunrise, on Sunday morning just before the water for the coffee starts to boil.

There is a continuous coming and going. A man wants to sell me a house, just in passing, so to speak. Indian women lay out wonderful woven cloths for sale. Basketwork furniture, toys, clothes, scarves, canaries, back issues of magazines, parrots — everything, literally everything, can be bought at the house door.

What a bazaar! And what bargaining and badgering! The shoeshine man finds his way in, collects all the dirty shoes and polishes them to a mirrorlike gloss while sitting on the sidewalk. He is also an essential industry, for it is easier to go without trousers in Mexico than without highly polished shoes. The man with the newspaper cart rattles by. The lottery-ticket seller offers sure wins that run into the millions. The itinerant shoemaker sits down on the sidewalk opposite the shoeshine man, last between his knees and materials strewn around him, hammering away and singing of his loved one who has left him and of his *ay ay ay* mortal grief. The shoeshine man joins in the refrain. The servant girls beating carpets on the balconies also feel themselves dying of grief. *Ay ay ay* — the whole street sobs and sighs, sings and weeps. The sun shines, the parrot in the neighboring garden squawks, the children shout and the street hawkers call. What a spectacle! What a city!

In "The God of the Two Rabbits"

Foreigners from lands where fermented grape or barley juice is drunk are in truth unlikely to develop a taste for *pulque*. They seldom have an opportunity to drink it, for it is not served at any of the better restaurants in Mexico City or Guadalajara. *Pulque* is the blessing of the poor, and their curse.

When street lights are turned on along the boulevards and avenues of the metropolis, *pulque* starts to work its effects in the less lovely districts. The slatted wickets of the *pulquerías* swing back and forth like the batwing doors of Texas saloons to admit the men, while women are served through a window near the door. For a few cents the laborer seeks euphoria or oblivion in dives with such poetic names as "The Agave's Tears of Pleasure," "Pyramid of the Hens," "Paradise of Eternal Peace," "The Line of Fire," "The God of the Two Rabbits," and "Debauchery Before Death." There is as little of paradise to be seen in these saloons as there is of pyramids of hens. A pyramid of cochroaches is much more likely to be encountered. These friendly little animals, known as *cucarachas*, chase each other across the mud floor of the *pulquería* as if they, and not the topers, were in a fit of "debauchery before death." Soon enough, however, the drinkers start the same game, get caught in each other's line of fire, bludgeon and knife each other, and end up as cases for the police and the ambulance crews, the last to leave the "Paradise of Eternal Peace." The Mexico City administration gradually has been closing large numbers of *pulquerías*. On the other hand, one reads with astonishment that the Mexican government is encouraging the cultivation of agave. Not everything that flows from the unpretentious agave is harmful *pulque*. The maguey agave is actually a harmless and useful plant that thrives in arid volcanic soil, protecting it from erosion, and producing commercial fibers. A long time is necessary before its juice can trickle through thirsty Mexican throats.

It takes eight years for the agave to grow from a little potted plant to a shrub six to nine feet high. In the full bloom of its eighth year, however, the stem of the agave is lopped off, and into the bowl formed by the hollow stump flows the *aguamiel*, the honey water, from the surrounding leaves. Twice a day an Indian siphons this honey water into a calabash and carries it back to the *rancho*. For five to six months the plant yields about five quarts of nectar daily. Then the agave is dead and withered, and a new seedling must suck its nourishment from the stony ground for another eight long years, until it too is decapitated.

It is for the sake of the honey water, not of the *pulque*, that the Mexican government promotes the cultivation of the maguey agave. In the dry season the children drink this honey water, which is said to be even more nourishing than actual honey. For the *ranchero*, however, whose maguey plantations stretch for miles across the barren uplands, the honey water is not an end in itself. After being brought to the ranch, it is poured into a steer hide or a pigskin that stretches to ten times its normal size with the weight of the liquid. Within twenty-four hours the honey water has fermented to *pulque* in its leathern vat, and after being poured into barrels the milk-white agave alcohol finds its way into the drinking halls with the idyllic names.

Modern Mexico has declared war on the traditional *pulque*, and here again the guiding principle of "reason before tradition." And it is indeed a long-standing tradition that is being broken, for *pulque* is as old as Mexico itself. The god Ometochli presented it as a treat to the Mexican children of Job, and the Toltecs and Aztecs got drunk on it. Aztecs, incidentally, were allowed to drink only on important feast days, and then only when they were past middle age. Pulque possessed an entire mythology. A mother goddess of the maguey had four hundred *pulque* children who lived in eternal delirium tremens. Each of the four hundred junior *pulque* gods, who inhabited the Moon in the form of white rabbits, was responsible for a particular stage of drunkenness. When one of the Aztecs had reached fifteen or twenty rabbits, he was considered merry. With forty rabbits he was tipsy, and the full four hundred rabbits stood for complete, abysmal drunkenness that could be punishable by law.

The pothouse keeper, who knew his classical legend and named his *pulquería* "God of the Two Rabbits," meant well. Two rabbits hardly correspond to a small beer. But the police expelled the god; the white rabbits had looked like white mice to the guests just a little too often.

A Bus Ride, Now That's Fun!

The bus halts at every street corner if a would-be passenger waves it down — and if the bus driver hasn't, on his own initiative, taken a different route because he can't stand a particular intersection. You pay the driver four cents for first class or three cents for second class, light up a cigarette, and hope that you're on the right bus, something you never can be sure of.

With sovereign composure the driver now grinds into gear, also lights a cigarette, hums an accompaniment to the *mariachi* music on his portable radio, peels an orange, briskly corrects the man behind him who claims that *El Negro* shot the equalizing goal against Guadalajara, wins a drag race with a colleague in a green bus, and slams on the brakes at the next traffic light so hard that sombreros slide down over sleepy faces. Two passengers wind up on the floor, but nothing is amiss.

At this point the bus is boarded by street hawkers, who trample on the passengers' toes. *Ultimas Noticias, La Extra, La Gráfica,* the evening newspapers, their print still wet with tomorrow's sensation, flutter over the rows of seats. *Chicles, chicles.* The six-year-old Indian girl dips into her bag and proffers chewing gum that her father and brothers have wrested from the hellish jungles of Yucatán. Serial magazines, funny objects, sweets and candies in every color of the rainbow are sold during the halt at the intersection. The lights turn yellow, and the street peddlers dive out of the bus. On we go apace.

The man with the guitar climbs in at the next traffic light and exchanges glances with the driver who continues to collect fares, makes change, smokes, eats, jokes, makes eyes at a pretty servant girl, grinds the gears, stamps on the gas pedal, and dashes on. We are in his hands again. The man with the guitar steadies himself in the aisle, plucks the strings of his instrument, shuts his anguished eyes — yes, that too — and raises his voice in song. He stands there unperturbed and sings like an early edition of Mario Lanza in this lunging, bucking, rattling knacker's cart. The man with the guitar sings through two bus stops, collects copper coins up to the third bus stop, exchanges glances with the driver — *Gracias*. We're off once more.

At the next stop he reins his vehicle — can buses rear up? — six inches from the zebra stripes so sharply that even the Black Madonna of Guadalupe on the windshield goes white with fear. *Andale, ándale mamacita.* Come along, little mother. He waves the old woman over the crossing with the noble gestures of a patron. *Caramba!* No time to be lost.

I alight at the next roundabout in the *Paseo de la Reforma*, at one of the six monumental, traffic-obstructing *glorietas* that seem to have been invented for the express purpose of discouraging candidates for a driving license. After a quick glance at the monument depicting the Aztec hero Cuahutémoc being tortured by Cortéz, I wave down a *pesero* taxi. The driver had been indicating with his outstretched index finger that he still had a seat vacant. Hundreds of *peseros* pick up and deposit riders all along the main thoroughfares of Mexico City. One can ride from the "Fountains of Diana" to Zócalo, a distance well over four miles, for one peso, or less than ten cents. Hence "*pesero,*" the one-peso taxi.

The Wedding Musicians

No European or North American fancy-dress ball is complete without this familiar Mexican costume: a high-crowned and usually black hat with a wide brim; a short, tight-fitting jacket; a brightly-colored neckerchief, narrow-fitting trousers with ornamental buttons down the seams, and elastic-sided boots. Every article of clothing is richly embroidered with silver. Now when Mexicans dress this way, they are either going horseback riding or serenading. Since the Mexicans actually do both incessantly, no tourist need ever leave the country feeling that the locals were hiding; the "typical" Mexicans in *Jalisco* costume will not elude the tourist. Nor he them, for that matter. If he strolls, for example, down the *San Juan de Letrán* of Mexico City to Garibaldi Square, a couple of minutes away from the *Torre Latino-americana*, he will scratch his head and wonder if Metro-Goldwyn-Mayer is making its two-thousandth film about Mexico. An impressive crew of extras is standing around, sombrero after sombrero, braid, lace, and embroidery in wasteful extravagance. Only these Mexicans are equipped with musical instruments instead of pistols. Before the tourist can ponder any further over this peculiar armament, the *mariachis* take him captive.

Mariachi is the bowdlerization of the French word "mariage," a wedding. At the time of Maximilian's arrival in Mexico, French culture was in the ascendancy, and this name became attached to groups of musicians engaged for all weddings and the more sumptuous rural feasts. Today among the most Mexican of institutions, buttress of *mexicanissimo*, these merry musicians seem to sing only of unhappy love and desperation, death, melancholy, separation, and abandonment. According to a musico-sociological theory, it is the unhappy memory of Spanish misdeeds that has given inspiration to these folk songs. Whatever their source, the *canciones rancheros* are really popular. Mexico City's thirty-eight radio stations broadcast them all day long, interrupted only by commercials for Coca-Cola, Alka-Seltzer, Tequila Sanza, and other similar necessities of life. The songs can be heard in the marketplace, at the airport, or at night in the streets when some gallant is having his *Palomita* serenaded. Anyone can engage the *mariachis,* just as in the days when the profession was founded.

The group makes a ring around the tourist, and the leader expresses his overpowering urge to entertain him with a serenade. It costs but ten pesos per song, and for this the orchestra may even include a symphony.

The tourist yields and sits down on a bench to enjoy the concert. Something *típico*, perhaps? The conductor, spokesman, and lead vocalist gives a sign, and a heartrending lament rises to the heavens. *Ay, ayy, ayyy.* The band sobs and howls like paid mourners. The red-brown face of the lead vocalist creases to an image of Agamemnon's tragic visage. With stentorian tones the "afflicted one" assures the world that he is suffering in silence — *pobre de mi / sufro en silencio.* The violins weep, the guitars mourn, and after every verse the musicians wail their long, drawn-out *ay ayy ayyy.* A picture of hopeless distress.

The tourist is impressed and requests another piece. This time he is prepared for what follows when the conductor tells him he will now perform the "Prisoner's Cry," *el grito prisionero.* But under the weight of all this collective grief, the band, the singers, and the bystanders threaten to collapse. What is suffered here is indescribable: *Te quiero, te quiero / este amor no puede mas callar / nadie ma me importa / jamas / te quiero.* The facts are clear. The prisoner loves a maiden, and testifies that nothing more will ever have any meaning for him. Never. The musicians sob out a last *ay, ayy, ayyy.* The voices expire, old before their time from sorrow. Their eyes dim with unspeakable grief, their copper cheeks suddenly sunken, they urgently need a shot or two of *tequila* for quick recovery.

Yet another one! In his euphoric state, the tourist hears, one after the other, how a young gallant, rejected by his sweetheart, fills the sea with his tears — *voy a aumentar los mares con mi llantó;* how a lad disembowels himself with a dagger, and all because of Maria, Maria, *Mariquita mia;* how a disappointed lover seeks forgetfulness in *pulque,* but finds only tears — *borracho me voy para olvidarte.* When the leader proposes to let the guitars burst into tears — *guitarras, lloren guitarras* — the tourist thanks him, pays, and goes his way.

He won't be missed. There are always visitors to Garibaldi Square. From early morning till past midnight the square before the church of St. Catherine is a musical maelstrom, a cacaphony of incredible dimensions, an acoustic madhouse. More than forty bands are blowing and strumming for their audiences, often all at once. They have to form circles around their individual listeners to seal them off with a wall of sound against competing influences. Very often these audiences don't even get out of their cars, but enjoy the serenades through the open car windows, then pay and drive off. Newcomers arrive. The *mariachis* welcome them — to a vivid land, to a vital country. Truly, *"Como México no hay dos."*

The plates

1. View of Ixtacihuatl (left) and Popocatépetl (right) across Mexico City

Lying 7,349 feet above sea level is the largest checkerboard in the world: the Mexican capital, *México D.F.* Here the Spaniards introduced for the first time the basic principle of their town planning, the grid, whose pattern later was to govern the layout of even the smallest villages of their American Empire. Not only the layout but the position is typical of a Mexican settlement. Mexico City spreads across a valley and is dominated by the two snowcapped volcanoes, Popocatépetl (17,887 feet) and Ixtacihuatl (17,342 feet).

According to the folk legend Popocatépetl (Smoking Mountain) was a prince who adored the Princess Ixtacihuatl (White Lady). When White Lady rejected a proposal, the prince first turned her and then himself into a mountain. The twin volcanos are thus perpetual monuments to this tragic love affair.

2. The University Library, Mexico City

Mexico's presidents provide for their immortality during their lifetimes. Between 1952 and 1954 President Miguel Alemán spent around fifty million dollars in building a university which probably has no equal in the world. Eighty thousand students attended the university in 1966. Tuition is only $18 a year, and the rush for entrance is so great that the university will soon be unable to cope with the situation. The first rector of the university once compared this colossal educational complex to an elephant that had been won by a poor family in a circus lottery! The National University is a miraculous achievement, both in architecture and in painted frescoes. The massive library was decorated by Juan O'Gorman with symbols from the ancient Mexican cultures. The statue in the foreground of the picture portrays the founder, President Alemán. The resemblance to Stalin was so remarkable that the sculptor had to do some retouching.

123

3. Paseo de la Reforma, Mexico City

Modern Mexican architecture has created an imposing slowplace for itself along this street. Its daring skyscrapers defy both the earthquakes and the shaky, unsteady terrain, which architects compare to a sponge cake. In the foreground of the picture are the *glorietas* that divide the traffic which all but chokes the city (in 1966, 450,000 vehicle licenses were issued). Not only avante-garde architecture is to be admired in the *Reforma*. From the equestrian statue of Charles V, the famous *Caballito*, past the Columbus and Cuauhtémoc Memorials to the Liberty Angel of the Independence Memorial, the traffic circulates around protagonists of Mexican history. The origin of *Paseo de la Reforma* begins with Emperor Maximilian, who, according to tradition, wanted his consort Carlotta to have the opportunity of following him with her eyes from Chapultepec Castle until he had reached the city.

4. The Zócalo with the Cathedral, the National Palace, and the City Palace, Mexico City

When Hernán Cortéz had captured the Aztec capital, Tenochtitlán, he immediately razed the temples of the gods. On the foundations of the Teocalli (temple) was built the largest cathedral in America (1573–1667), which occupies one side of the *Zócalo*, properly called the Square of the Constitution (*Plaza de la Constitutión*). The *Zócalo* is one of the largest squares in the world and is the center of the capital. On Sunday evenings the buildings around the *Zócalo* are illuminated by floodlights that show

at its most impressive the colonial baroque that the pupils of José Churriguerra made into the style of Spanish America.

5. In Chapultepec Park, Mexico City

Chapultepec Park on Sunday is the playground of the people. There are shady spots for picnics, a zoo, an amusement park, walks, and riding paths. Those interested in culture can find the Modern Museum, the National Museum of Anthropology, and the brilliantly arranged Museum of National History. Here, on the "Locusts' Hill" of Tenochtitlán, are the royal tombs of the Aztecs. A Spanish viceroy built a castle here, which was later occupied by Maximilian. The city lies at its feet, together with the huge parks that serve as the lungs of *México D.F.*

6. One of Diego Rivera's Frescoes in the National Palace, Mexico City

Mexico's modern painters have been muralists and, ever since the revolution, have just about covered the country with their enormous frescoes. The historical themes they depict are the colonial era, which is portrayed as a period of oppression and exploitation, the greatness of the pre-Columbian civilizations, and, above all, the glorious revolution with its heroes and martyrs. These are the motifs that the muralists painted and still paint everywhere on the walls of town halls, banks, theaters, movie houses, universities, hotels, libraries, and railway stations. The hard realism needs no interpretation

124

or translation. Everyone understands the message of Rivera, Orozco, Siqueiros, Tamayo, and O'Gorman. The picture shows a fresco by Diego Rivera in the National Palace that portrays a scene from the Aztec capital, Tenochtitlán.

7. Tlaltelolco, Mexico City

In the center of the ultramodern residential complex of Nonoalco-Tlaltelolco lies the Square of the Three Cultures. The oldest church in Mexico, the Church of Santiago, rises above the pre-Columbian ruins of Tlaltelolco and is itself dominated by the new foreign ministry building. An amalgam of three eras, civilizations, and ways of life has been created, which is described on a memorial plaque in front of the Church of Santiago: "On 13 August 1521 Tlaltelolco fell into the hands of Hernán Cortéz, having been heroically defended by Cuauhtémoc. This was neither triumph nor defeat. It was the painful birth of the *mestizo* people that is today the people of Mexico." In the Square of the Three Cultures, Indian Mexico has been reconciled with the Spanish heritage, and both have united to form modern Mexico.

8. In the Museum of Anthropology and History, Mexico City

If this museum were not intended as a history book for a people that has a certain degree of illiteracy, it could stand as a model of modern architecture and museum arrangement. Its halls, its inner courtyard,

and "the largest suspended roof in the world," which hovers 88 feet above the inner courtyard, are architectural marvels. Twenty-five halls cover 52,624 square yards and contain about ten thousand archaeological finds, which range from a ten-ton stele to the filigree work of the Zapotec silversmiths that is smaller than the finger of a newborn baby. Maps, photographs, films, and reconstructed models supplement the excavated fragments and make an easily understandable picture.

9. Celebration in Honor of the Virgin of Guadalupe, Mexico City

The most important holiday of the Mexican Catholics takes place on December twelfth. Tens of thousands of pilgrims stream to the Basílica of Tepeaca (above) to pray before the reliquary of the Virgin of Guadalupe. The many pilgrims, who often come hundreds of miles on foot, surround the basilica with a cacophony of celebration. Hour after hour the Indians from the mountains perform their ritual dances in honor of the "Brown Virgin" until they collapse from exhaustion. The feather headdresses, the robes, and insignias of heathen antiquity are now only worn for "the greater glory" of the "Patroness of America."

10. Los Remedios

The Spanish upper class had only contempt for the Indian religious spectacles and the Virgin of Guadalupe. Their patroness was the "Virgin of Remedios," whose statue is supposed to have been placed by Cortéz on the altar of a heathen temple. The statue was lost, but later found again by natives working in a maguey field. The statue vanished on two other occasions, but was recovered each time. This was interpreted as an expression of the will of the Holy Mother that a church be built. The feast day of the Virgin is celebrated by the Indians on September eighth in Los Remedios near Mexico City with ancient religious dances.

11. Xochimilco

The "Floating Gardens of Xochimilco" are the surviving reminder of the time when Hernán Cortéz found the "Venice of the New World." The freshwater canals and lagoons of Xochimilco still provide the capital with part of its drinking water and also water the vegetables and flowers that overflow the markets of *México D.F.* in boundless plenty. Xochimilco is quite popular among local people, as well as foreigners, as a place for excursions. Swaying gently over the shallow canals are hundreds of flat-bottomed boats hung with garlands, flowers, and flags in that blaze of color so beloved by the Mexicans. *Mariachi* musicians, snack bars, and restaurants are all a part of delightful Xochimilco.

12. Mariachi Band in Front of the Church in Tepozotlán

"There are two things in Mexico that I will never understand," said an English diplomat. "What the contents of a *molé* sauce are, and when a *mariachi* musician sleeps." These musical groups can be heard at almost any time of day or night and one sees them literally everywhere – for instance, in front of the church in Tepozotlán, as in the picture. This church has been a museum since the revolution, and the buildings in the surrounding area have been restored in the style of the colonial era. The church architects Correa, Ibarra, and Cabrera have created a masterpiece of colonial baroque in Tepozotlán.

13. Sculpture on the Temple of Quetzalcóatl, Teotihuacán

The archaeological zone of Teotihuacán measures about six square miles and is divided into various "districts," which run south from the Pyramid of the Moon to the so-called Citadel. The entire area of the temple city was once paved with a kind of cement, and the surfaces of the pyramids are also overlaid with cement slabs. The largest of these pyramids is the Pyramid of the Sun, with a base 138 feet square and a height of 207 feet. The Pyramid of the Sun consists of five pyramids rebuilt on the same site, and the Temple of Quetzalcóatl (shown in the picture) is also a construction of piled-up pyramids, each built for the sacred fifty-two-year cycle.

14. Hacienda La Gavia

Not far from Toluca, the capital of the state of México, lies the little town of Zinacantepec.

One of its first mayors had built the Franciscans a monastery there and had received from the king the gift of a large estate as compensation: the Hacienda La Gavia. For four hundred years the estate was in private hands, and among its proprietors were many famous figures of Mexican colonial history. Today, La Gavia is a *pension*, a place for excursions and weekend meeting point for the inhabitants of the capital, as are many other illustrious mansions. Here also the tourists pay for the preservation of a beautiful old estate, which would otherwise have been ruined by revolution and decay. Many *haciendas* are surviving by means of this compromise. They are emerging from the centuries-old Spanish exclusiveness and adjusting themselves to modern Mexico in a democratic fashion.

15. Morelia

Morelia (110,000 pop.) the capital of the state of Michoacán, is beautifully situated amid captivating scenery. The city was originally called Valladolid, and acquired its present name from the national hero José Morelos, who was born here and worked in the town as a parish priest and teacher. Morelia's cathedral was built between 1640 and 1744 in the colonial style of that time. In the southern section of Morelia, the church *"Las Rosas"* (shown here) has been preserved in the same style, and in this church sings Mexico's most famous children's choir, *Los Niños Cantores de Morelia,* directed by Miguel Bernal Jiménez. The city is particularly proud of its two-hundred-year-old aqueduct, which was built at the initiative of a bishop who wanted to make sure the city had a water supply and also wanted to alleviate the unemployment problem through public works.

16. Cactus-Covered Landscape Near Ixmiquilpan

The Mexicans have conferred heraldic honors upon the cactus by incorporating it in their national coat of arms and displaying it on their flag, their money, and their state seal. The cactus is to be found everywhere, and Alexander von Humboldt once wrote: "The cactus shape is peculiar to the new continent, sometimes round, sometimes divided into limbs, sometimes standing upright in high polygonal columns like organ pipes." There are around 850 kinds of cactus and the versatility of the plant is proverbial. The *peyote* cactus provides a narcotic, but from many other kinds of cactus different medicaments are extracted. The cactus is used as a totem, as firewood, barbed wire, clothesline, fruit juice, and knitting needles. Even the cactus louse supplies the world with cochineal, a rare red dye.

17. In the Capilla del Rosario at Puebla

Puebla (322,000 pop.) is one of the richest and most beautiful of the colonial-style cities in Mexico. Since its founding in 1532 the city was controlled by the Spanish clergy, not only spiritually but commercially. The ninety-five churches, some ornamented with unimaginable magnificence, are of this era.

The so-called *Churriguerrismo* in church architecture reaches its climax here. This style of baroque was extremely popular in Spanish America, and is named after the Madrid architect José Churriguerra (1650–1723). He employed the most extravagant ornamentation: wreaths, spirals, balustrades, garlands, obelisks – which, combined with the Indian sense of color, achieved lavish optical effects, as here in the *Capilla del Rosario*.

18. Harvesting the Maize on Ixtacihuatl

Maize, or Indian corn, is even more typical of Mexico than the cactus. According to the Toltec Genesis, man was created from maize, which was called "the grass of the gods." With its cultivation the Indians became settled and abandoned their wanderings, so that maize can be considered a basic factor in their development of civilization. For thousands of years the maize cake, the *tortilla*, has been the staple food in Mexico. With different types of stuffing, the *tortilla* yields the principal Mexican dishes: *tamales, tacos, enchiladas,* and *quesadillas*. Steamed or boiled maize is eaten right from the cob. *Atole* is a maize drink, and the fermented grain yields "*pulque de maís.*" Sowing and harvesting are still religious ceremonies in many places.

19. The Pyramid of Niches in El Tajín

In their temple city of El Tajín the Totonacs built pyramids in the niche style, which was here more distinctive than anywhere else in ancient Mexico.

The 365 niches (a sacred number and the number of days in a year) are arranged like rows of windows in seven stories. The religious significance of the niches is still a mystery. El Tajín was the capital of the Totonac Empire from about 600 to 1200 B.C. The city went into decline when the Totonacs were driven out in the course of the general migrations, but they founded a new religious and political center in Cempoala.

20. The Ocotlán Shrine in Tlaxcala

This place of pilgrimage is an excellent example of colonial baroque. The pomp of the *Churriguerrismo* culminates in the *retablo facade* (retablo: altarpiece) with ornate gables and columns decorated with ornaments in the form of garlands. If baroque is accepted more as an expression of vitality than as a style of art, then Latin American church architecture is proof not only of the wealth of the Spanish feudal society but of its need to demonstrate this wealth with pomp and display.

21. The Portal of the Cathedral of Chihuahua

Chihuahua (170,000 pop.) is the capital of the state of the same name. This state is Mexico's largest and richest. The largest herds of cattle graze on its prairies, its mines are the most productive, and its forests yield the greatest returns. The capital is the most important communications and business center in northern Mexico. In this city the notorious revolutionary hero Pancho Villa was born. His memorial, the town hall, and the baroque cathedral are worth a visit, as is the nearby picturesque mining town of Aquila Sedam.

22. Monterrey and Saddle Pass

In 1900, Monterrey, the Mexican "Mountain of the Kings," had 72,000 inhabitants. Today almost a million people live in the capital of Nuevo León. With modern iron- and steelworks, lead foundries, and other kinds of metalworking, Monterrey is the center of Mexican iron and steel production. After a series of reverses due to drought and floods, the Monterrey "boom" was unleashed in the 1930's by the brewing industry, and the town hasn't looked back since. Monterrey is probably the most "American" city in Mexico. The picture shows the *plaza* and the cathedral; in the background is the characteristic silhouette of Saddle Pass.

23. Landscape near Tequesquiápan

The earth of Mexico can be as dry as the sand from Pandora's box or as stony as the rock to which Prometheus was manacled; it is very often a combination of both. The landscape is seldom kind to man and is never gentle, but is always stimulating. Despite a lack of water, some plants can flourish where no crops could ever hope to grow. Cactus and agave drive their taproots through the earth's hard crust and store up a mouthful of bitter water for the thirsty traveler.

24. Guanajuato

In such fabulously wealthy silver towns as Taxco, Zacatecas, Querétaro, and Guanajuato, the spectacular architecture of the colonial era reached its zenith in the seventeenth and eighteenth centuries. These towns bear glittering witness to a glittering era. Guanajuato (34,000 pop.) is a town in the pure colonial style whose palaces and stonework are held to be the most subtle refinements of *Churriguerrismo*. Guanajuato paid for its splendor with the yield of one of the most famous silver mines in the New World, the *Bonanza Valenciana*. As far back as 1803 Alexander von Humboldt wrote of this project as "the greatest and boldest enterprise in the history of mining."

25. In the Cañon del Cobre

The *Sierra Madre Occidental* in the south of the state of Chihuahua contains a system of gorges and canyons that is one of the most enormous and least explored in the world. *Cañon del Cobre* (Copper Canyon) is one of the least accessible of these canyons. In this area live the Tarahumara Indians, almost completely undisturbed by the outside world. They are famous for their stamina in running and climbing. A Tarahumara can travel 124 miles per day, and needs only a mouthful of maize and a swallow of water for nourishment. An impressive scene in Mexico City's *Ballet Folklorico* is of the Tarahumara hunting a stag, and depicts an actual chase on foot until the deer's strength begins to flag and a hunter can run close enough to shoot his arrow.

26. Weavers from the Mezquital Area

27. Potter in Tlaquepaque

Three states are famous for their handicraft: Oaxaca, Jalisco, and Michoacán. Oaxaca specializes in weaving, ceramics, and metalworking; Michoacán in wonderfully refined lacquerwork; and Jalisco in all of these. Tlaquepaque, a suburb of Guadalajara, is to a certain extent Mexico's handicraft capital. Here bast- and leatherwork are produced, and silversmiths, glassblowers, and weavers work with age-old patterns and methods. The potters, however, outdo all of the others, and have turned Tlaquepaque into a gigantic warehouse of jugs, pots, vases, masks, beakers, chandeliers, and figurines. Judged by its often high artistic value, the pottery can be obtained very cheaply, but is not always easy to carry away as souvenirs.

28. Charro Festival

Like the Texas cowboy or the Argentinian gaucho, the Mexican *charro* embodies a glorified past and typifies perhaps the most original form of Mexicanism *(mexicanidad)*. The *charreria* is today the most popular status symbol of the Mexican upper class. In Mexico City, Guadalajara, Puebla, or Querétaro, the fashionable thing to do on Sunday mornings is to go riding on the trotting paths, rigged out in what most foreigners erroneously believe to be the Mexican's everyday costume: an enormous sombrero, tight trousers and jacket, and broad belt

with pistol holsters – all of which is embroidered and inlaid with silver. A *charro* outfit costs a small fortune, and it is quite understandable that those who have one like to show it off on religious and national holidays, in harmless equestrian sports, and during the *paseo*.

29. Guadalajara

When Mexicans or their friends from abroad join in praises to the country "that is like nowhere else," the name Guadalajara recurs again and again. The "Queen of the West" has often been praised in song, along with Jalisco, of which Guadalajara is the capital. In 1965 the population of the city exceeded one million. Guadalajara lies at an altitude of 5,180 feet and has a wonderful climate, like an eternal spring. It is the second largest industrial center in the country, after *México D.F.* As proud as they are of their breweries and shoe and textile factories, the "Tapatíos" are even prouder of their romantic reputation, the uninterrupted Spanish way of life, and the countless magnificent buildings of the colonial era. The city extols itself as the "imperishable symbol of our Mexicanism" – and with justification.

30. El Salto

Right on the border between the states of San Luís Potosí, where Mexico's first productive oil well was drilled, and Tamaulipas, where most of the oil is extracted today, lies a place that is famous, not for its oil, but for its water: El Salto, the waterfall. It is not without justification that this cataract is called simply "The Waterfall"; it is Mexico's most famous. Its vicinity can be recommended to conservative anglers who have no desire to go harpooning for swordfish or sharks, and the surrounding countryside is known as an excellent hunting ground. Even the peaceable nature lover will find his efforts well rewarded once he has the dusty side road of the F 80 (between Huizache and Antiguo Morelos) behind him. A little inn, Las Cabanas, can probably serve the angler what bad luck or ineptitude had deprived him of at the Salto.

31. The Patio of the Hacienda Vista Hermosa Near Cuernavaca

Mexico's social order was feudal. The church and the Spanish aristocracy divided between them an enormous amount of landed property, and a private *hacienda* could be as large as 296,400 acres. The *hacienda* was the focal point of the landed empire, and generally reached or even exceeded the size of a village. The owner's house was often decorated and furnished with considerable splendor. Vases and chandeliers from Venice, valuable Oriental carpets, richly carved furniture and chests, rare books, paintings, costly works of art, and holy statues bore witness to the power and grandeur of their owner. The photograph shows the inner court of the Hacienda Vista Hermosa, which was built by Cortéz and serves today as a hotel.

32. Palace of Cortéz, Cuernavaca

Cuernavaca lies almost 3,300 feet lower than Mexico City and is the fashionable weekend and summer resort of the capital's high society. Hernán Cortéz recognized and appreciated the perpetually mild climate of Cuernavaca and built for himself a summer residence. The building is heavy and ponderous – it was fortified – and far from the flighty baroque of the generations to come. To make the Spanish summer residence Mexican, Rivera decorated it with a fresco that depicts all the horrors of the *conquista*. Hernán Cortéz, commemorated by not a single monument in Mexico, could not even be allowed to rest in peace here.

33. The Cathedral, San Miguel de Allende

Several towns vie for the right to be called the most beautiful and architecturally pure of the original Spanish colonial settlements. That the government has decided to declare San Miguel de Allende a protected national monument is proof enough of the pure colonial character of this town of 16,000 people. Nothing may now be altered in the center of the town; only interior renovations are allowed. San Miguel de Allende is colorful and idyllic. Its streets are steep, narrow, and paved with cobblestones. The houses and their *patios* are decorated with the gaily colored Puebla tiles, and the atmosphere is medieval Spanish. Even the cathedral has an architectural style more reminiscent of Gothic than of the more usual colonial baroque.

131

34. Stone Figures at the Temple of Tula

The very existence of the Toltec's royal city of Tula was disputed by scholars until 1940. The ancient Tollan of the Toltecs was held to be nothing more than legend, a sort of Atlantis or Utopia, and the accounts given by the baptized Toltec Prince Alva Ixtlixochitl were dismissed as fairy tales. In 1940, however, the remains of Tula were discovered near the little town of Tula de Allende. The temple city was founded in 767 and destroyed by the Chichimecs in 1040. The Toltecs are admired as mathematicians, mechanics, and architects, and it was they who introduced the column into ancient Mexican architecture. These so-called Atlas columns in the form of sixteen-foot-high caryatids at one time supported the roof of a temple.

35. Market in Taxco

Anyone who wants to meet the people in Mexico should go to the market, for to the Mexican the market is more than a place of business or distribution. It is an essential element of life and has a social function. This is where opinions are given, bargains are struck, discussions are held, food is broiled or roasted and then consumed, the local drinks are drunk, music is played and songs are sung, the people work, sleep, beg, quarrel, laugh, and tell tall stories. One should take time off to have a good look; it is stimulating, since there are few things between heaven and earth that cannot be found in a Mexican market. Flea markets, clothing stalls, picture stalls, jewelry stalls, and God alone knows what other kinds of stalls are spread out beside the usual markets, where tropical foods of all types are displayed.

36. Taxco

Taxco is another protected national monument and also vies for the honor of being "the most beautiful city in the land." Taxco's fame stands on a base of silver. One is inclined to exaggerate and claim that everyone in Taxco is a silversmith. At any event, seldom is so much silver piled in one place. The man who really silverplated Taxco was José de la Borda, the richest man of his time. He is said to have minted forty million silver *pesos* from the *Bonanza* of Taxco. Borda invested a considerable part of his fortune in the building of Taxco's cathedral (in the background of the picture). It became one of the most magnificent churches in Mexico, and Borda had kept to his motto: "God gives it to Borda and Borda gives it back to God."

37. Monte Albán

At 1,312 feet above the Valley of Oaxaca is the artificial plateau on which the Zapotecs built their pyramid city of Monte Albán. Archaeologist Alfonso Caso, who is in charge of the excavations, called the Zapotecs "A people of master builders," and Monte Albán exhibits their monumental creative power. The Zapotecs removed the mountain peak and constructed a pyramid and temple city about one-half mile long and one-quarter of a mile wide. They not only created monumental edifices but were perhaps the most skillful gold- and silver-smiths of ancient Mexico, and brought miniature and fine chased work to a perfection that was never achieved by their successors.

38. Fishermen on Lake Pátzcuaro

If we didn't already know that the fishermen of Janitzio, the island in the background of the picture, have always caught the delicious *pescado blanco* with their butterfly fishing nets, then we would be convinced that they were fishing in Lake Pátzcuaro on behalf of the local Chamber of Commerce. Here, however, we will find that picturesque scenes are commonplace – the butterfly dance of the boats, Janitzio with its steep, narrow streets, and pastel-colored fishermen's houses, the nets hung up to dry, and the yellow floral offering and silent torchlit procession to the cemetery on the eve of the "*Día de los Muertos,*" Mexico's All Saints Day.

39. On the Beach at Acapulco

The "Street to Asia" ended in Acapulco or, rather, it began there. Acapulco was for centuries the port, customs station, and place of transshipment for the goods that arrived from the Spanish Philippines. The goods were then transported overland to Mexico City and Veracruz, and from there were taken to Spain. Use of Acapulco as a port declined steadily after the collapse of the Spanish overseas empire. When an American and a Mexican bought up almost all the beach property in 1934, they were thought to be out of their minds. They paid 15 cents per square yard and the whole transaction cost them $35,000. Today the beach of Acapulco is worth hundreds of millions of dollars, and the dirty little fishing village has become a sophisticated bathing resort – probably the most sophisticated in the Americas.

40. Acapulco

This celebrated resort has 80,000 inhabitants and 500,000 tourists a year. Most of the tourists, about 85 percent, are Mexicans, who lodge in unassuming little boarding houses. The other 15 percent are the international playboys and playgirls of the "Jet Set," the "Beautiful People," the "Ins" who give Acapulco the lustre of a luxury vacation paradise. They are Texas oil millionaires, New York divorce lawyers, Milan bankers, Paris fashion princes, and Spanish bullfighters, with the complete retinue of cover girls, Hollywood starlets, and beauty queens from the four corners of the earth.

41. Washerwoman Near Acapulco

The glittering beach boulevards of Acapulco run directly into the mountainous country of Guerrero, one of the wildest and most violent of the Mexican states, where the mountain villages seem to be light

133

years away from the "Pearl of the Pacific." Electricity, running water, and even roads are almost unknown in Guerrero, but not washdays. For time on end women from the vicinity have used the river ford as their open-air laundry.

42. Flowers

The flower seller with his handcart brings a moving flourish of color into the markets of Mexico City. His assortment of blooms usually contains the traditional roses, carnations, tulips, jasmine, orchids, and gladiolas. These flowers, and many others whose names are of Indian origin, are piled into resplendent mountains in the markets. Even ancient Mexican civilizations were obsessed with flowers, and made floral offerings to the gods.

43. Fruits

Even more abundant in the markets than the Indian flowers is the profusion of fruits. In miniature pyramids are heaped oranges, limes, lemons, melons, plums, pineapples, avocados, tomatoes, pears, capuli cherries, mangoes, and camotes. Bunched beside them are sugarsweet bananas as small as an index finger, and dark-brown cooking bananas like big bludgeons. At least half of these fruits are almost unknown to the American palate as are the dozens of different sorts of chile peppers that are offered for sale: black, red, green, yellow, brown and violet, mild, sharp, and hot as hell, like the Tabasco chile that the Indians call *xocoxochitl*.

44. The Monastery Church of Santo Domingo, Oaxaca

The state of Oaxaca still has a population largely Indian. Fourteen Indian tribes speak fourteen different languages, and on market days and religious holidays when the Indians crowd into the state capital, also named Oaxaca, a veritable scene of noise is the result. The feast of Santo Domingo, who is particularly venerated in Oaxaca, takes place on August fourth and the city is flooded by the country people. A magnificent monastery in the capital has been named after the saint, and the Indians take part in the pilgrimage to the monastery church. Others participate in a Mass at one of the villages of Oaxaca which have Santo Domingo as their patron saint: Santo Domingo Ixcatlán, Santo Domingo Roayaga, Santo Domingo Tomaltepec, and Santo Domingo Zanatepec.

45. Mitla

The Zapotecs and Mixtecs are the most important of the fourteen tribes in Oaxaca. They are direct heirs to the advanced civilizations which had their capitals on Monte Albán and in Mitla. Mitla, the "Abode of the Dead," was not a place of sacrifice or a religious center as was Monte Albán. It was a residential town where the kings and high priests lived and now lie buried. Of the four great palaces in Mitla, the "Erectheum America" is the best preserved, and it has been restored. The Spaniards built a church in the inner courtyard of the palace "to break the magic of the heathen religion."

46. The Kukulcán Pyramid, Chichén Itzá

Calling this temple "El Castillo" (The Castle) is deceiving because the temple of the feathered serpent, on top of the pyramid, was never a residence but a shrine. The Kukulcán Pyramid contains remnants of eight smaller pyramids. The Maya reckoned time in cycles of fifty-two years, and when this "end of world" period came to an end they razed the old temple and from it built a new one. In one pyramid a life-size jaguar (an animal venerated by the Maya) of red stone overlaid with jade was found.

47. On the Beach at Cozumel

Only a few years ago Cozumel was a forsaken little spot in the Caribbean Sea. Today this island is a playground for the international set, and has the advantage of being exclusive and almost unspoiled. In its tropical forests parrots still flutter and squawk almost undisturbed, gaudy hummingbirds flit from petal to petal, and lianas and wild orchids grow in unrestrained profusion. The even, sandy beach and the lagoons on the western side are just two of the attractions of this resort.

48. The Fortress of Campeche

The privateers of the Caribbean Sea lay in wait off Panama and Puerto Cortéz, off Veracruz, and off Havana and Santo Domingo for the treasure ships of the Spaniards. They burned down the cities along the east coast of Mexico and robbed and plundered in the names of English and French rulers. Dutchmen, Danes, Italians – they all tried their hand at this rewarding pastime. English freebooters even founded their own colony, British Honduras. The Spaniards constructed coastal fortresses to deter the insolence of the pirates, and the fortress of Campeche developed into one of the most important harbors on the east coast of Mexico. Since the treasure ships usually sailed for the New World without cargo, the Spaniards loaded them with marble ballast, and with this marble the public buildings in Campeche and many other Mexican towns were constructed.

49. The Nuns' House, Uxmal

In the middle of the Yucatán rain forest lies Uxmal, the ancient capital of the New Maya Empire. A visitor once said: "Uxmal radiates a harmony, due not only to its symmetry but also to an aura of the Golden Age." Thirteen temples and palaces stand on pyramids and terraces. The Prince's Palace is monumental and richly ornamented. According to tradition, the consecrated temple maidens lived in the Nuns' House.

50. Palenque. The Governor's Palace

Palenque in Chiapas was one of the cities that were ruled by despotic priest-princes during the Maya feudal era. Comparable in power with the European Sun Kings and perhaps even more powerful than they, these priestly castes had created theocratic states where they themselves occupied the place of the gods on Earth. These priests were the astronomers and mathematicians that we still admire today; nevertheless, they were not natural scientists as we understand the term in the western world, but rather astrologists. They attempted to fathom the divine laws and intentions through the magic of figures. The course of the world depended on their decisions, their power was absolute, and they guarded their knowledge from the people as a secret and privilege. We are still unable to decipher completely the Maya script, which was a secret script only for the initiated, but we can take our bearings from the rich frescoes of the temples and palaces, which are among the most impressive edifices of the ancient American civilizations. The Governor's Palace of Palenque also indicates the degree, power and extent of the theocracy. The palace is still larger than, for example, the Temple of the Sun, and is set off by a tower which probably served as an observatory.

PHOTO CREDITS:

Hermann Grathwohl: Cover, 1, 2, 3, 5, 7, 9, 10, 11, 12, 13, 14, 15, 16, 18, 23, 26, 27, 28, 35, 36, 38, 39, 40, 41, 42, 43, 44, 47, 48, 50 / Horst v. Irmer: 4, 6, 31 / Werner Jünger: 8, 33 / Walter Reuter: 17, 19, 20, 21, 29 / Enrique Franko Torrijos: 22, 25, 30, 45 / Pontis-Photo-Jaenicke: 24, 46 / Ilse Steinhof: 32, 37 / Detlef Hecker: 34.

Printed in Germany. 167.

DATE DUE	

Pocket Inside

MEXICO   Political Map

Names of cities over 1,000,000 are capitalized
National capitals   MÉXICO CITY
Secondary capitals   Mérida
Secondary Boundaries   Railroads

0   50 100   200   300 Miles
0 100   200   300   400   500 Kilometers

COPYRIGHT BY
RAND McNALLY & COMPANY

Longitude West of Greenwich